BE A HERO
AT YOUR OWN WEDDING

When it comes to planning weddings, there are tons of books and magazines to help the bride with decisions big and small—while the groom is left groping along in the dark. Now *The Groom's Survival Manual* steps into the breach with down-to-earth advice on:

- The ring—buying a nice one without getting ripped off
- In-laws—keeping them out of decisions you want to make with your bride
- Controlling the guest list—or how to make sure some bozo doesn't show up with an uninvited date
- What the groom pays for (traditionally)
- Dealing with the minister, priest, or rabbi—what to expect from pre-marital counseling; planning the ceremony; paying the officiant
- Coping with cold feet—remember: your single buddies secretly envy you, no matter what kind of wisecracks they make
- Enjoying the big day—looking good on the reception line, the dance floor, and more.

The trip from "Will you?" to "I do" doesn't have to be a hassle. Let *The Groom's Survival Manual* show you the way, and check into the wedding suite without checking into the asylum.

THE
GROOM'S
SURVIVAL
MANUAL

Michael R. Perry

POCKET BOOKS

New York   London   Toronto   Sydney   Tokyo   Singapore

An *Original* Publication of POCKET BOOKS

POCKET BOOKS, a division of Simon & Schuster Inc.
1230 Avenue of the Americas, New York, NY 10020

Perry, Michael R.
    The groom's survival manual / Michael R. Perry
        p.   cm.
    ISBN 0-671-69357-3
    1. Wedding—United States—Planning—Handbooks, manuals, etc.
I. Title.
HQ745.P38   1991
395′.22—dc20   91-8758
                                                  CIP

First Pocket Books trade paperback printing June 1991

10   9   8   7   6   5   4

Design: Stanley S. Drate/Folio Graphics Co. Inc.

POCKET and colophon are registered trademarks of
Simon & Schuster Inc.

Printed in the U.S.A.

For Cynthia,
*the bride who made it
so much fun to survive.*

SEPTEMBER 1989
LOS ANGELES

ACKNOWLEDGMENTS

Special thanks must go first to my sister Claudia, who suggested the idea. Thanks also to J. C. Hearsch, for help with the legal chapter; to Patricia Viamonte, for valuable research assistance; and to Gavin and Kathy, who read the first draft and liked it so much they decided to tie the knot themselves. And thanks also to Roger and Janet Perry, a.k.a. Mom and Dad, for their unflagging moral support.

CONTENTS

1

SO YOU
REALLY DID IT

A man who chooses to get married is a man of action: a guy who knows what he wants and won't take no for an answer.

So you went and fell in love. And for once in your life everything seems to be going right, catching you completely off guard. Since *she's* been around, food tastes better, colors are brighter, and people are noticing the extra bounce in your step, commenting on how happy you appear. Whereas before you debated whether life's glass was half full or half empty, since you met her you feel that the glass is positively overflowing. Fortunately, you had the depth of character to realize that something so unbelievably good happens only once in a lifetime, and that you should take some action to preserve the magic. You asked the woman of your dreams to marry you. Congratulations on your engagement! Unlike many men who don't know what they want, you have the wisdom and resolve to capture the initiative and start traveling the path toward real happiness and satisfaction.

Moving from the bachelor mind-set into thoughts of marriage can often be a scary leap of faith into the unknown. Like anyone making a major decision, every potential groom has stayed awake at night imagining the arguments for and against his course of action, until at one instant his whole being is transformed and he realizes that he wants to share his life with the woman he loves. There are no more arguments for or against; the only questions remaining are how and when. The man who decides to get married is a man of action; he has taken the ball into his hands and is running with it.

The mystery of women explained with the assistance of modern science.

Now the only hurdle between you and married life is the wedding. You thought it would be pretty simple. *No problem . . . I pop the question, and then several months later we go to the church and exchange vows. Bingo! I'm married.* What most grooms are unprepared for is the interval between "Will you?" and "I do." As soon as the engagement is announced, self-appointed wedding experts appear from out of the woodwork, like genies from Aladdin's lamp. With only the best of intentions, these experts want to dictate the "proper" way to handle every detail of your wedding, from the wording of your invitations and vows down to the kind of cheese you put on the crackers at the reception.

The bewildered groom soon recognizes that in the world of social protocol, planning a wedding is only slightly less complicated than planning D-day. The bride has a staggering array of resources at her disposal, instructing her in the proper execution of every maneuver. There are fourteen books and six magazines with the word *Bride* in their titles, all chock-full of information and advice; chances are, your fiancée has already become quite an expert on the subject herself. And the groom? He's just supposed to know.

WHY IT'S IMPORTANT TO BE A GOOD GROOM

It can be tempting to throw in the towel and take the attitude, "Just tell me what to do, and I'll do it." You may think that the fuss surrounding the wedding is silly and incomprehensible, and that the only important thing is the success of the marriage, but such an attitude fails to recognize that working with your future wife during the planning of the wedding can influence the marriage. The way you do things as a couple between now and "I do" can set patterns of communication that will grow over the course of your marriage.

The groom's role in the wedding is almost always smaller than the bride's, yet he needs to diplomatically participate as much as possible in every phase. Getting married is a *public* affirmation of commitment between a man and a woman, and weddings are a volatile mix of emotions, religion, legal issues, family issues, and the transition from living as a lone wolf to being a part of a team. The groom who actively participates learns a great deal about himself, his wife-to-be, both of their families, and the manner in which all of the interested parties will interrelate for years to come. The groom who just says "get me to the church on time" can find himself playing catch-up.

Once he realizes the enormous value of taking an active role, the shrewd groom needs to develop strategies to accomplish dozens of intermediate goals. What am I supposed to do? What am I supposed to pay for? How do I deal with my in-laws? My single friends? My clergyman? There is a long list of things that grooms are *just supposed to know about.*

On your own, you have to buy an engagement ring and wedding ring; draw up guest lists for yourself and your family; plan the honeymoon; find a best man and ushers; pay for a variety of symbolically important wedding expenses such as the bride's bouquet, a gift for the bride, and the officiant's fee; and so on. Constantly asking your fiancée and her entourage of wedding planners what you need to do is the worst way to go about it. You'll be seen in a far better light if you cheerfully surprise them by fulfilling your role before being asked: *The tuxedoes? I've notified all the ushers where to go, their measurements have been taken, the right clothes are on hold for the wedding date, and I've arranged for the best man to return mine to the shop.* The man who is always prepared and knows what to do (and when) generates a certain larger-than-life mystique, and your fiancée and her family will rightly believe they can depend on you.

THE SUPPORT ROLE

More important, you have to provide encouragement to your fiancée as she accomplishes a much longer list of goals. She'll have to work with "wedding professionals" such as florists, catering services, and photographers; she'll have problems with her own family and their demands; and she'll probably have those bad days where the amount of work seems to outweigh the romance. What you can do is just be there for her. Even if you share all responsibilities as a couple, there will be days when your fiancée is simply overwhelmed. By just listening and sympathizing you can begin to establish yourself as the team player you know you are.

The overambitious groom needs to guard against becoming too involved; there is a fine line between taking part and getting in the way. The traditional wedding is hosted primarily by the bride's family, and the bride is the center of attention. Although many couples take charge of their own weddings, and others split up duties along nontraditional lines, it's still very likely that your bride wants this to be *her* day. Watch your fiancée and listen to her wishes, and do an excellent job of discharging your own responsibilities. If she wants your input on other subjects, help out enthusiastically; if not, try to stay out of the way.

KEEPING YOUR SENSE OF HUMOR (Without Making Fun of Your Own Wedding)

Marriage is a wonderful institution; a wedding is a wonderful thing; and yet, planning a wedding can be a remarkably demanding gauntlet. There has evolved over the last one hundred years "the wedding industry," which has little to do with love, commitment, or compassion. The wedding industry is comprised of caterers and jewelers and dressmakers and printers and forty-piece bands, all of whom want to convince you that only *they* can make your ceremony and reception truly special, and that whatever they want to charge (no matter how high) is fair and equitable. You need to realize pretty quickly that some of these helpful people are nothing but sharks who want to prey on your insecurities. The special thing about your wedding is that you and your fiancée will exchange vows. Everything else is packaging. *Whatever you and your bride want to do is the right thing.* "Experts" will tell you that the "proper" way to do something is to buy the product or service that they're selling. Listen to the "experts," then do whatever you want. If you and your fiancée want more than anything else to get married on a roller coaster, then go ahead and do it. *The wedding belongs to the bride and groom,* not to all the "helpful" specialists.

Even if you're having a traditional wedding in a church or temple (as does the majority of couples), and a reception with music, food, and drink, the planning can occasionally become trying. Just remember that no matter what hoops you have to jump through, the goal is worth the effort: You will be marrying the woman you love.

2

MISSION
OBJECTIVE:
BUY A RING

Often, the first item on the groom's agenda is to give his fiancée an engagement ring as a symbol of their commitment to get married. This is definitely a classy gesture and has the added benefit of scoring big points with the bride, her female friends, and her mother. A pleasing feminine quirk is the way that a woman will walk around with her left hand extended for weeks after receiving an engagement ring, greeting old friends and strangers by waving her new bauble in their faces. This kind of appreciation can make any groom feel like a righteous dude and is ample reward for having chosen "the right ring."

"The right ring" is whatever you want to get her. Tradition dictates a simple "brilliant cut" (round) diamond on a gold band, but engagement rings can have any jewel, from a rhinestone to a rock rivaling the Hope diamond in scale, mounted in silver, gold, platinum, or copper, inexpensive or extravagant. Your fiancée will love any ring you choose.

However, she will love a diamond more. As Marilyn Monroe sang, "Get that ice or else no dice . . . Diamonds are a girl's best friend." Many grooms decide to take Monroe's advice seriously, and are confronted with a staggering array of choices, prices, and claims concerning diamonds and engagement rings. All they need to emerge from the diamond market with an unqualified victory is simply a little basic training and some good information.

11

If you want to surprise your fiancée with a ring, the first bit of classified intelligence you have to gather is her finger size. Marching into her home and asking, "What size is your ring finger?" dissipates the surprise, and she will immediately become suspicious and believe, correctly, that you intend to buy her a ring. This would not be the end of the world, but if you want to keep your objective under wraps until the day you pull the ring out of your pocket, there are covert methods to ascertain this information.

When you are visiting the home of the woman you intend to marry, wait until she is in the bathroom, on the phone, or otherwise temporarily indisposed. Invent a cover story for going into the room where she keeps her jewelry (in case you are discovered, a good alibi is, "Uh, I was looking for a book"), and stealthily pilfer a ring that she already owns. Place the purloined trinket in your pocket and escape undetected.

Later, visit a jeweler, making certain that you haven't been followed. Ask him to tell you what size the ring is. It does not have to be the jeweler you intend to buy the engagement ring from; any decent jeweler is able to determine the size of a ring. Write it down—otherwise, in the excitement of shopping you'll forget and may end up with a ring that looks like it's meant for her big toe. On a subsequent visit to your sweetheart's abode, create a diversion, and surreptitiously replace her ring in its original location.

Now that you've gathered the intelligence, you are prepared to embark on a journey into the dark world of consumer manipulation populated with despots known only as "jewelers." This is not meant to besmirch the reputation of the many honest jewelers in America, but the "bad apples" make it mandatory that a jeweler earn your trust before you do business with him. Be as skeptical about an unknown jeweler's claims as you would be about a used-car salesman's.

Chances are, the average groom does not have much experience with jewelry, and buying the engagement ring can make him emotional and easy to exploit. Jewelry salespeople know this, and have taken out full-page ads in national magazines implying that the size of the diamond that a groom buys is a measure of his love for his future wife. This jeweler's propaganda recommends that you spend "two months' pay" on your fiancée's engagement ring.

While an engagement ring is a romantic, admirable gift, it is *not* an indication of the depth of your feelings about your fiancée, nor is it a measure of your character, upbringing, or sincerity. Many despicable citizens, including armed robbers, drug dealers, liars, cheats, and heels, have purchased enormous diamond rings for their fiancées. On the other hand, many perfectly nice guys, who turned out to be fine husbands, did not spend two months' pay on an engagement ring. Diamond size does not equal good husband material.

"Two months' pay" is the jewelers' strategy to extract as much dough as they possibly can from anxious men. If you can spend a full year's pay on a ring, that's fine, and if you can afford only a token from a gumball machine, that's fine too. How much you spend is your personal decision and is related only to how much you can afford. You know how much you love your bride-to-be, and you know how much you want to spend. Those facts have no relationship to each other, no matter how many full-page ads the diamond syndicates take out.

Once you've decided of your own free will to buy a diamond engagement ring, you will have to contend with jewelers in order to buy it. First, determine how much you want to spend. Whether it's $150 or $150,000, setting a budget is a way to keep yourself from fixating on a ring that will put you deeply into debt.

Doing a little research shows that the same quality diamond in the same type of setting can be found for prices that vary by as much as 300 percent. That means you may find a certain ring for $500 which, on the other side of town, sells for $1500. The standard retail mark-up on diamonds—that is, the difference between what you pay and what the jeweler paid—is about three times. Therefore, be prepared to haggle somewhat over the price, the same way you would when shopping for a car.

How can you tell that you're comparing prices on the same

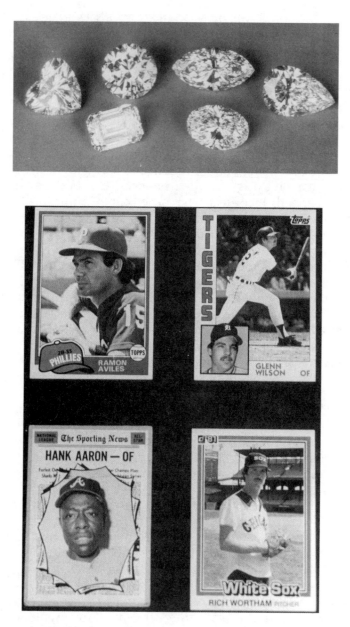

Distinguishing a valuable diamond from a clunker is as difficult as identifying a collectible baseball card. Can you tell which is which?

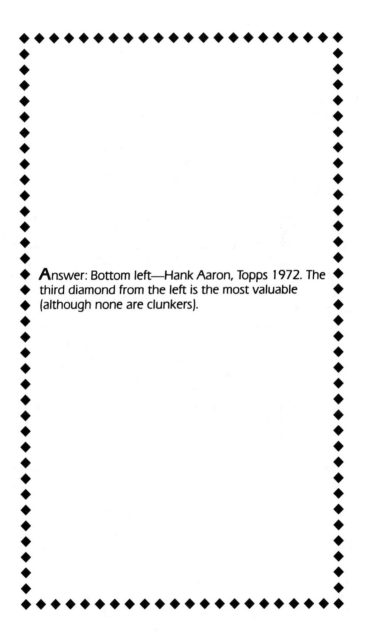

Answer: Bottom left—Hank Aaron, Topps 1972. The third diamond from the left is the most valuable (although none are clunkers).

kinds of jewels? Buying diamonds is a little cryptic, and distinguishing between a good one and a bad one is a little like finding a valuable baseball card—it takes some knowledge beyond casual examination, as on first glance they all look pretty much alike. Essentially, there are four measurable factors that determine the market price of a diamond: carat weight, color, clarity, and cut.

Carat weight is the most commonly known diamond statistic and refers to its size. A carat, for those scientifically minded, is equal to 200 milligrams, or 3.086 grains. Another way to think of it is that there are 142 carats to the ounce. When buying diamonds, it's enough to know that, all other characteristics being equal, a heavier diamond is more expensive. Diamonds are measured in carats and fractions of carats, so you will see diamonds that weigh .47 carats (a little under half a carat), 1.14 carats (a little over one carat), and so on. Familiarize yourself with this terminology and remember that carat weight alone does not determine price.

A little-known tip when diamond buying is that prices go up sharply at near the .80 carat weight. Jewelers "bracket" the prices around the whole-carat marks, and they consider a .80 carat diamond close enough to 1.00 carat to round the price up. Similarly, a 1.80 carat diamond will be valued like a 2.00 carat diamond, and so on. If you're looking for a lower price, look at a .75 carat diamond instead of a .80, or a 1.75 instead of a 1.80. The small difference in size will probably not be noticeable, but the money you save may be substantial.

Conversely, if you're flush, you may be able to find a considerably larger diamond for approximately the same cost. If you have the cash to buy a .80 carat diamond, you may find that a 1.00 carat diamond is not that much more expensive, and represents a better value for the money spent. The secret is knowing at which point the price goes up.

Color is the second diamond characteristic to consider. There are "better" and "worse" colors, and jewelers have complex charts that evaluate color status. There are presently at least five different methods for classifying color, including the old-fashioned names such as Jager, River, and Wesselton,

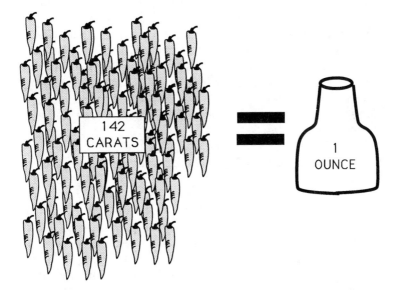

The **carat** is simply a unit of measurement, like the ounce, the pound, or the kilogram. It has nothing to do with that healthy vitamin A–rich vegetable, the **carrot.** There are 142 **carats** to the ounce. Diamonds are sold by the **carat,** whereas **carrots** are typically sold by the pound.

which originated from the locations where diamonds were mined in India, to the English system of Blue White, Finest White, and so on. Some large jewelers, such as Tiffany's, have even cooked up their own nomenclature for color classification, so getting the straight dope can become very difficult.

Fortunately, most jewelers in America either use or recognize the classifications of the Gemological Institute of America. If your chosen store uses a different system, ask them to translate it into a GIA designation. The GIA assigns letters of the alphabet to colors, beginning at the letter D (why they didn't start with A is puzzling, but it's easy to remember, since *diamond* begins with D). It's very important when doing comparison shopping to know what GIA color code has been given to the rock you're looking at.

A D color designation is reserved for the very finest jewels in the world, which are known in England as Blue White and are extremely rare and expensive. Z is called Dark Cape in England, is visibly yellowish, and is cheaper. Everything else falls in between. The D end of the spectrum is for hard-core collectors who like to split hairs over color, but the untrained person cannot detect much color in a stone all the way down to an L classification. Ask to see examples of different-colored diamonds. Chances are, you can find a stone you like in the middle of the scale and avoid paying for status you can't discern.

After carat weight and color, the next characteristic determining a diamond's value is clarity. The diamond's ability to reflect light is impaired by imperfections in the stone, which can include carbon specks, bubbles of nitrogen, internal cracks, or cutting imperfections. A jeweler uses terms such as *inclusions, clouds, feathers,* and *butterflies* to describe imperfections, but the buyer need only know the GIA's clarity grade in order to comparison shop effectively.

The GIA clarity grade is standardized like their color designation, and your jeweler should tell you the exact clarity code of a diamond you intend to buy. It begins with FL, for Flawless Diamonds, which contain no imperfections that can be detected with a 10x power jeweler's loupe. It goes down from there to VVS (Very Very Small spots), VS (Very Small spots), all the way down to an I_3 diamond, which is obviously marred.

Flawless diamonds are for collectors and Elizabeth Taylor, and a few small flaws are hard to detect. The average person usually can't find any flaws down to a VS_2 designation, so again, ask your jeweler to show you stones of the various grades in order to pick one that is to your liking but isn't unnecessarily expensive.

Cut is the only diamond characteristic put there by human beings and, except in the case of a badly miscut diamond, is largely a matter of taste. Brilliant cut stones are the traditional round shape, which reflects the most light through the stone. Oval and heart-shaped diamonds are also popular. The number of facets, or flat edges, on diamonds comes from their cut. Facets help make the diamond sparkle.

Armed with all this information, it's now possible to shop for a good price on a diamond. Let's say one jeweler shows you a .45 carat, K color, VS_2 clarity, brilliant cut diamond that you like. You can now shop for similar diamonds at other retailers, and be assured that you are comparing apples to apples, until you find a price you feel is fair.

Since most grooms cannot tell whether the salesman is telling the truth about all these arcane statistics, find a jeweler you can trust and who knows his craft. The best way to find an honest dealer is through the personal recommendation of a friend or relative. In addition, a diploma or certificate of course completion from the Gemological Institute of America indicates that the jeweler has had formal training in the field. Since anyone can open a store and call himself a gemologist, and since most states have no certification requirements, choosing a formally trained jeweler at least indicates that he is knowledgeable. Ask to see proof of his training—it's a fair request when you plan to plunk down a large sum of cash in his store. If a jeweler won't demonstrate that he's had recognized training, go elsewhere. There are plenty of jewelers in the world who will. A good jeweler should explain through demonstration the traits of a particular stone and answer all your questions in plain English.

FINDING AN
HONEST JEWELER

Tomorrow morning, you could purchase a stock of jewelry, put a sign on your door, and call yourself a gemologist. Most states have no licensing requirements. When shopping for an engagement ring, you may encounter someone who has done just that. Try to get a recommendation from a customer of the jeweler. Choose a jeweler who has been in business long enough that you can reasonably expect him to be there if you have a problem. Ensure that the jeweler has had formal training and is willing to explain difficult terms to you.

Disreputable jewelers may try to play on your naïveté. Be extremely wary of the following:

1. Any jeweler who claims to have "flawless" diamonds probably doesn't know his craft or is lying. Virtually all diamonds have imperfections, and those that are truly flawless are extremely rare and expensive.

2. Claims that a diamond is Blue White are also to be considered with suspicion, and will probably come from the same dealer who said he had flawless jewels.

3. "Wholesale to the public" is a contradiction in terms and very likely just a gimmick. Real jewelry wholesaling is only from one dealer to another, generally in bulk. A retailer who claims to offer wholesale prices may be selling inferior jewelry. Ask for the statistics on a jewel, and compare it to the price of a similar jewel at another retailer. His "wholesale" price may be higher than a more reputable jeweler's retail price.

4. The quickest way to spot an unprofessional, untrained dealer is if he pronounces a VS_1 diamond as "Vee Ess *Eye*." The correct pronunciation, which any trained jeweler would know, is "Vee Ess *One*."

Once you've selected a stone and found the best price, you need only to pick a setting. This is largely a matter of personal choice, and jewelers should be able to show you a wide range of bands to choose from. One consideration is that if your fiancée is a surgeon, sculptor, or otherwise uses her hands frequently, you should choose a shorter setting, so it doesn't get in her way. This is also the time to pull out the paper with her ring size on it (aren't you glad you wrote it down?). There is a small risk that the ring you swiped was not her correct size, and the one you're buying won't fit. Ask the jeweler for a written guarantee that he'll resize it for free if necessary. Also, request a certificate guaranteeing that the stone is the size, color, and quality he told you it was. Reputable jewelers will be happy to comply with both requests.

Having emerged from the world of jewelers intact, all that remains is for you to give your fiancée the ring. You can be direct and just fork it over, or you can be creative in the presentation. John Vance, an Ohio groom, popped the question on Christmas Day, and hid the ring in an ornament on the Christmas tree. Other fun ways to give your fiancée a ring include dropping it in a glass of champagne when making a toast, leaving her notes that send her on a scavenger hunt to find it, and slipping it on her finger when the two of you are holding hands. Methods that are *not* recommended include burying the ring in a plate of spaghetti, tying it to a rock and throwing it through her window, or shooting it at her out of a gun. Assuming you don't do anything rash, any method of presentation is sure to be appreciated.

If you were happy with the service you got from your jeweler, you and your fiancée can go back together to choose wedding bands. When you shop together, she'll be extremely impressed with your expertise on the subject of jewelers and jewelry. Don't tell her you learned it from a book. Just let her believe you're very smart.

3

TEAM
GROOM

When organizing the massive amount of labor that a wedding requires, the bride and her family are the joint chiefs of staff, and the big decisions, the overall strategies, and the bulk of the responsibilities often (but not always) fall to them. However, the bride's division is dependent on you, the groom, to assemble a crack team of highly specialized commandos to accomplish some minor but critical objectives. *Team Groom* consists of you, your family, your best man, and your ushers, and it's up to you to ensure that they execute their missions flawlessly.

YOUR FAMILY

Under some circumstances, the families of both bride and groom share all responsibilities equally. Especially if her family lives out of town, if she is not emotionally close to them, or if the bride is an orphan, then the groom's family can find themselves responsible for a larger share of the wedding responsibilities or even for virtually everything.

Their Support Role

More likely, your family will act in a support role to the bride's organization. They should write to her parents soon after the engagement is announced, offering *assistance*, not *suggestions*. Creative control is always retained by the bride, but the groom's family can assist either with finances or labor, to any degree agreed upon by them and the bride. Like the groom himself, his family must be careful not to cross that fine line between helping out and getting in the way.

THE REHEARSAL DINNER

The groom's family traditionally hosts a *rehearsal dinner*. As the name suggests, this shindig is held after the wedding rehearsal. You can help coordinate this event with your parents. Many grooms opt to have the rehearsal dinner in a restaurant, or have it professionally catered, although if your parents live in town and can handle the crowd, the rehearsal dinner can be held at their house.

At the least, the rehearsal dinner should include the immediate families of both bride and groom; the maid of honor, bridesmaids, best man, and ushers; and the officiant. Don't forget to invite the officiant! Your clergyman (or whoever will be doing the honors) will be working as hard as any member of the wedding party, and several weeks before, when the rehearsal dinner is planned and a head count is taken, it's easy to forget that one vital invitation. Especially after the officiant presides over the rehearsal, it would be pretty rude for everybody else in the party to leave for a fancy dinner without including him.

Ideally, the rehearsal dinner is small, and provides an opportunity for those in the wedding party to catch up with one another before the rigorously scheduled wedding day. There are no hard and fast rules about who should and should not come, so if there are out-of-town guests or close friends who are not part of the "official" wedding party but whom you would like to have attend, feel free to invite them. Check with your bride to see if she has any special guests she wants included.

If the rehearsal dinner is to be held at a restaurant, be sure to coordinate with the establishment as early as possible. Restaurants usually cannot handle a group the size of a typical rehearsal dinner without some planning. Visit the establishment, and try to find a separate room or secluded section of the restaurant where the group can be seated apart from casual diners. During your research phase, try to eat at the restaurant of choice at least once. Oftentimes a place with great decor has little else to offer, and no quantity of crystal chandeliers and silver dinnerware can compensate for a steak that should have been made into a pair of hiking boots.

Ask the restaurant to make some special concessions for your group. since this is a once-in-a-lifetime meal, it's not unreasonable to ask them to rearrange the tables in a circle, T shape, or U shape, so that all the guests can see one another. If you want to dictate the seating arrangements, deliver cards with your guests' names on them, and give the maître d' a diagram showing which name goes where. It is also incredibly hip to arrange for fresh flowers on the table—and perhaps a single red rose at the bride's seat. You can ask the florist who is preparing the bridal bouquet to deliver flowers to the restaurant the day of the rehearsal.

Try to schedule the dinner to begin as soon after the rehearsal as possible. Since the event is usually held the night before the wedding, it should not drag on too late into the evening. Ask your clergyman how long the rehearsal will take, add an hour for travel and unforeseen circumstances, and make the dinner reservations for that time. For example, if the rehearsal starts at 5:00 P.M., and the clergyman estimates it will take 90 minutes, make the dinner reservations for 7:30 (5:00 plus 90 minutes' rehearsal plus one hour for errors and travel equals 7:30).

Budget for Rehearsal Dinner

Your family is responsible for picking up the check at the rehearsal dinner. If you'll be ordering off a menu, find the cost of a typical entrée, add the cost of a couple drinks, coffee, and dessert, and then add 15 percent service charge plus the local tax to arrive at a cost per person. Having the event catered (banquet style) instead of letting guests order off a menu can make the costs more predictable, but be certain that there will be enough variety to satisfy your guests. It's nearly inevitable that someone will be on a diet, someone else won't eat meat, and someone else just hates chicken. Even if you choose banquet-style dining, you still need to add in the price of drinks and gratuity to arrive at a cost per person.

YOUR FAMILY DURING THE CEREMONY

Your family's role during the ceremony depends on religion and tradition but is generally smaller than that of the bride's family. The bride is traditionally "given away" by her father, who walks down the aisle with her, but the groom walks alone, his parents having been seated before the ceremony begins. If you and your bride want your parents involved in some way during the ceremony, ask the officiant. He may be pleased to let parents read scripture, or become involved in some other way, and your parents might welcome the offer to participate. Although it is not traditional, the father of the groom occasionally acts as best man (see below), in which case he will perform all the duties expected of that role.

TEAM GROOM

Your best man and your ushers form the core of your support unit, and it is critical that you coordinate their efforts within the overall wedding strategy. The best man can be a friend, your brother, father, uncle, or cousin. The best man should be someone you are close to and upon whom you can depend. At the least, he is charged with keeping you sane on the wedding day, and he can also throw a bachelor party, take charge of the rings, participate in some aspects of the ceremony, and sign the wedding certificate. In addition, he will probably escort the maid/matron of honor at the prewedding celebrations and at the reception.

The ushers are significantly more important than their lowly title indicates. In addition to seating guests at the wedding, they attend the bachelor party and often stand at the front of the church during the ceremony. The usual formula for deciding how many ushers are required is one usher for every fifty guests; however, the critical determining factor is how many ushers your *bride* wants. In a formal wedding, she will want as many ushers as there are bridesmaids, regardless of the number of guests, so ask your bride before you start making your list.

Once you know how many men are to be on your team, you can fill the list from your close friends and family members, and even men from your fiancée's family, if you so desire. Although the father of the groom is occasionally the best man, he is rarely an usher. Finalize your choice of groomsmen in plenty of time for them to select formalwear and to adjust their schedules to attend your wedding, especially if some will be coming from out of town. Be sure that all ushers attend the rehearsal.

You should designate a "head usher" to coordinate the others' efforts on the day of the ceremony. The ushers should arrive at the church at least an hour before the ceremony, fully dressed, washed, sober, and ready to seat guests. They also should know who has special assigned seating—usually the families of the bride and groom, as well as guests who are wheelchair bound. Beyond that, the bride's family and friends are seated on the left side of the church and groom's family and friends on the right. If one group is grossly outnumbered by the other, this little rule should be quickly tossed out and guests escorted to the next available seat.

Technique

Ushers stand by the door, and as each group arrives, an usher should politely inquire whether they are the bride's or the groom's guests. The usher then offers his right arm to the senior woman of the group and leads her to an appropriate seat, with the others following her lead. If a single man arrives, he is taken to his seat without the benefit of physical contact (*"Follow me, sir"*).

The second to last to be seated, regardless of when they arrive, are the mothers/grandmothers/great-grandmothers of the groom, followed by those of the bride. The head usher should handle this special formality. Once they are all seated, the groomsmen assume the formation they learned during the rehearsal, and the ceremony begins.

Team Groom at the Reception

Your best man begins the reception with a toast to you and your bride. After the bride and groom dance alone, the best man dances with the maid/matron of honor, and the ushers dance with the bridesmaids. If you encounter resistance (like a whiny "but I don't know how to dance!"), it is up to your best man to whip the stragglers into shape.

Gifts

At the bachelor party, or at the rehearsal dinner, the groom traditionally gives gifts to the ushers and the best man. As much as you might like to give them *Def Jam Classics Volume IV*, it is more appropriate to give something traditional and personalized, like a tie tack with their initials, a classy pen, or a monogrammed flask. Usually the gift for the best man is a little nicer (read: more expensive) than those for the ushers. Personalized gifts take at least a couple of weeks to prepare, so start shopping early. Good places to find that "special something" for Team Groom include men's sections of department stores, tobacco shops, formal-wear retailers, and fancy catalogs.

By carefully and thoroughly taking charge of Team Groom, you give your fiancée and her family one less thing to worry about. Even though you have fewer responsibilities than your bride, they are crucial pieces of the overall puzzle, and staying on top of them will once again show them what a resourceful, clever, and dedicated fellow you really are.

4

THE INVITATION LIST: YOUR FIRST FIGHT?

The invitation list: Your first fight?

UNREALISTIC EXPECTATIONS

When Garth, a 26-year-old police detective from Columbus, Ohio, got engaged to Vicki, a legal clerk, he had in the back of his mind images of wedding receptions from television shows and the movies.

From Princess Di to "Dynasty," every wedding Garth had ever seen had included hundreds of people, plenty of food and drink, and receptions held in luxurious ballrooms with forty-piece bands. The day after "popping the question," he had informed the whole police force that they would be invited, as well as his high-school graduating class and his favorite bartender.

A couple of weeks later, when Garth met Vicki's family to discuss the wedding, the detective uncovered a couple of uncomfortable facts: First, unlike television weddings, where nobody ever gets a bill, the expenses for his wedding were going to be paid by Vicki's family; second, Vicki and her parents wanted the ceremony to be in Pittsburgh, where their family lived.

After Garth and Vicki left her parents' home, he launched into a diatribe, complaining that she had made too many plans without consulting him and she had destroyed his whole vision of a perfect wedding. Vicki countered that Garth had been the one to jump the gun and pointed out that he shouldn't have told so many people they'd be invited without first asking her about it.

33

Garth dropped her off without kissing her good-night and that evening tied on a good drunk with some police lieutenants. The next morning he came to his senses and stopped by Vicki's house at dawn to make up. He spent the next couple of weeks explaining to Columbus's finest that no, they wouldn't all be invited. The next summer, Vicki and Garth were happily married in Pittsburgh, in surroundings somewhat less lavish than those shown on "Dynasty."

Even if you have a more realistic view of wedding costs and limitations, your friends, business associates, and acquaintances, especially the single ones who have never gone through a wedding, may still believe that yours will be a gigantic party to which everyone in the world will be invited.

Because someone has to pay, your wedding can't be infinitely big, and unless you're marrying Donald Trump's daughter, there will have to be a lid on the number of guests you invite. If you are footing your own bill, this harsh reality becomes much easier to understand, but if your bride's family picks up the tab, you may not fully understand the economic difference between fifty guests and five hundred. At $20 per person (a low figure) for food, drink, and a few frills, ten extra people adds $200 to the total.

Your mission, should you decide to accept it, is to negotiate for the number of friends and relatives that you can realistically invite, stretch your quota to include as many guests as possible, educate the ones who are poorly informed about wedding etiquette without offending them, keep out troublemakers, unwanted dates, and freeloaders, and help out-of-towners with their lodging needs so that you don't end up having thirty people fighting to sleep on your couch. Making an invitation list seems simple at the start but can turn into a full-fledged confrontation for the unprepared groom.

GUEST LIST NEGOTIATIONS

In the ideal world, the total number of guests is happily agreed upon by the bride, groom, and their families, and then the list

On television, weddings are always spectacular. Everyone is invited, lavish feasts are prepared, and no one pays a bill.

is divided fifty-fifty between the bride's gang and the groom's. Then again, in an ideal world the home team always wins. It's only when dealing with reality that difficulties arise and compromise becomes necessary.

Guest list negotiations can be as complicated as contract talks, and each party will have persuasive arguments supporting his or her case. A wedding is generally considered the bride's day, and she may feel that she should be allowed to invite anyone she wants, and she's right. The people who are paying (traditionally, but not always, the bride's family) may believe that they are entitled to control the guest list since they'll be getting the bills, and they're also right. The groom may think that since he's half of the reason for the event, he can invite whomever he wants, and he too is right. His family is right to assume that they should be able to invite important friends and close relatives.

The challenge is to bring all of these absolutely correct viewpoints to some sort of agreement without hiring lawyers. The problem is often exacerbated by the fact that before discussing the matter each negotiator has informally told a few people they'll be invited. When the first guest list is drafted, it's not uncommon to discover twice as many names as can realistically be included. This is where emotions might flare and a cold war can begin.

YOUR GUEST LIST

Before the talks begin, draw up a list of family and friends whom you'd like to invite. Think about your immediate family as well as relatives who are important to you. Consider current friends as well as buddies from childhood who were exceptionally close. Names of people from college, work, or military service can also go on this first-draft list. Don't get carried away, however; names should be drawn from your personal life. Including all the people from your job, or your plumber, mechanic, and favorite checkout person at the grocery is not advisable.

Then, in privacy, grade the people A, B, or C, depending on how important they are to you. If you're a libertarian or a Texan, you may feel it's pretentious to rate human beings, since "all men are created equal," but you're not making character judgments—just deciding how strongly you want them at your wedding. You should have three lists for negotiations: the short "A" list of everyone you "must" invite; the "B" list of folks who would be nice to see; and the "C" group of people you thought of but wouldn't necessarily miss.

If, when you approach your wife's family (or whoever else is paying), they say "Invite them all," enjoy marrying into the Trump clan and skip the rest of the chapter. However, if you *can't* get everybody in the door, you're ready for the bargaining table.

THE OTHER LISTS

Bring the three lists when you discuss with the others how big the wedding will be. You may know in your heart that the fifty-five souls you absolutely, positively must invite are your nearest, dearest friends, and to eliminate a single name will cause you great consternation. It's important to understand that your bride and both sets of parents feel similarly about their lists. It's just that all those names may add up to too many guests.

You may discover that you and your fiancée have radically different opinions of what the wedding and reception should be like. Throw in a couple of sets of parents and it could become a free-for-all. A good way to begin is by finding out what everybody's first-draft list includes, without considering costs. Maybe your parents want the "Dynasty" wedding, with free-flowing champagne and a forty-piece orchestra at the reception. Perhaps you find it most important to get married in a church and don't care so much about the reception. Your bride could have envisioned a more intimate get-together all around, and her parents may care most about seeing that her family will be able to attend.

After you know what's most important to all parties involved, discuss the knotty questions of cost and logistics. Often, families in different locales each assume the wedding will be in "their" town. Officially, the bride and her family have the final say, but understanding what everybody wants ahead of time can help optimize the resources. A common discovery is that there's not enough cash to please everyone, and the downscaling begins.

PARING DOWN YOUR GUEST LIST

When the gap between what's desired and what's possible has been narrowed, you should arrive at a bottom-line total number of guests who can attend the wedding and reception. The groom is supposed to be allocated half of the available slots, but don't be surprised to get less. That realistic count may be too low to accommodate even your "A" list.

Now comes the time to make cuts in your list. It's a difficult call to make, and if you've ever been cut from a football team, or not accepted to the college of your choice, you will recall the feeling of rejection you suffered at the time. To settle your mind, remember that you got over that rejection and lived to tell about it. People who don't get invited will survive, and except in the most extreme cases they will not stick pins through voodoo likenesses of you and your bride.

There is no sure system for cuts except to consult your own sense of judgment; however, there is an acid test for determining "close" friends. Look at each name and ask yourself: *Have I ever been invited to his (or her) home?* It's often enlightening to note how many supposedly close friends have never invited you over, and possibly never will. If nothing else, it should alleviate some of the guilt when you draw a thin, dark line through their names.

Once you've created a workable list, you have to get addresses with ZIP codes. If the filing system in your life consists of scraps of paper scattered all over the house, this may be difficult, but it's possible to get street addresses from the phone book and ZIP codes from the post office. Put all this information onto a few sheets of paper, photocopy them, and give the originals to your fiancée.

PADDING YOUR GUEST LIST

You probably want to invite a few more people than you'll be allowed, whether you've been allocated eight slots or eighty. A proven strategy in guest-list padding is to "guesstimate" the number of people who will actually show up once they've been invited. The important limit is on the number of guests who can *attend*, not on the number you send invitations to.

It's a little unorthodox to invite eighty people and count on only sixty to attend, yet this time-honored gambit will let you have your cake and eat it too: You get to honor family and friends by inviting them to your wedding, without the responsibility and expense of having them all show up. It would be cold-blooded to *hope* that invitees won't be able to make it to your wedding, but it's realistic to assume that not every out-of-towner will drop what he's doing and fly to your ceremony. You can probably think of several close family members or friends whom you'd like to invite but who, for reasons of age, finances, or schedules, will not come. Those people can safely be sent invitations. The clever calculating is for the people in the gray area: maybe they'll come, maybe they won't.

Determining the likelihood of whether someone will show up takes some serious figuring. You probably know who has the financial resources and time to travel a great distance and who doesn't. Both factors should be considered, as well as a knowledge of how important attending your wedding will be to them, and what sacrifices they'll make in order to get there.

Taking all these factors into account, the best way to dole out invitations to the "maybes" is to estimate the probability for each of them to show up. (Get out your calculator). If you have six relatives in Alaska, and you think that there's a fifty-fifty chance any of them will fly down, you can invite all six, and add only three names to your approximate guest list. Or, if you used to live across the state and have ten good friends in your old town, perhaps there's an 80 percent chance that they'll make it. If you invite them all, count on eight of them to attend.

The successful guest-list padder can invite quite a few more people than his official quota. The technique must be used judiciously, however, and you should still invite only those people who are important to you. Just because someone is far away and unlikely to attend is no reason to send him or her an invitation; don't order phone books from distant cities and begin addressing invitations to strangers who share your last name. Remember too that many recipients will feel that an invitation to your wedding is a social obligation to send a gift, whether or not they attend.

As clever as guest-list padding may seem, it can backfire if not used with caution. If you decide to invite your high-school swim team just because they live across the country, and the team captain charters a bus to drive them all out, you can't retract their invitations.

If you are not a gambler, or cannot think of a reasonable estimate for calculating who will actually attend, the "correct" method for padding the guest list is to send out first only the exact number of invitations that you are permitted. Whenever someone notifies you that he or she cannot attend, immediately send out an invitation to the next person down on your list. The disadvantage of doing this is that you may be sending out invitations very near the date of the wedding. Three weeks before the date of the event is about the latest that invitations should be received.

R.S.V.P.

R.S.V.P. is an abbreviation of the French phrase, *Répondez s'il vous plaît,* the literal English translation of which is, "Tell the gosh-dang wedding planners as soon as possible whether you're gonna show up at their gig." Even if "R.S.V.P." is not actually written on the invitation, it is the responsibility of the recipient to respond with a letter (best) or phone call (second best) indicating whether he or she will attend.

You'll discover that at least a few invitees do not read French, cannot comprehend the U.S. postal system well enough to write a letter, or do not have a telephone. Short of sending them an etiquette manual, there is no "proper" way to force them to respond. Although officially the responsibility is on the invitees to respond, if they haven't, you still need to root out the information to make an accurate head count and to pad your list further. A good way is to call these people a couple of weeks after sending out the invitations and ask, "I was wondering if you got the invitation. We haven't received your reply." This reverse–R.S.V.P. will help you fine-tune your guest list, even if it flies in the face of propriety.

PHONE CALLS FROM THE DEAD

Ring! Ring! Ring! You answer the phone, even though it's strange to get anything better than a wrong number at 2:00 A.M. A preternaturally chipper voice greets you: "Hey, dude, who do you think this is?"

Half-asleep, you search your memory. The voice sounds vaguely familiar, but you can't quite place it. You take a guess. "Ed McMahon?"

"Ha! Ha! You wacky, zany card! My buddy hasn't lost his sense of humor! It's Harvey!"

Your mind reels. You feel neither wacky nor zany. What's worse is that you have no idea who is on the line. Harvey? There is no Harvey in your life. "What number did you dial?" you inquire.

"My oh my, still the nutty prankster like the good ol' days. It's Harvey Dopslinger, your best pal from high school."

The haze clears a bit, and you vaguely remember a Harvey who sat in back of you in chemistry class, eight years ago. You rack your brain for details, hoping to remember the guy. Harvey Dopslinger. Wasn't he the one with the tape on his glasses? If that Harvey is the same one who just woke you up, he's certainly overstating his case in claiming that he was your best friend. The only time in the past such a casual acquaintance ever called was to sell you life insurance.

Friends you haven't heard from in years (or thought were dead) may call, asking for an invitation to the wedding.

FROM THE COLLECTION OF MARILYN GARDNER

"Gee, I've already got some coverage," you say, making the assumption that Harvey, too, wants to insure your life. Why else would he call after eight years?

"Yuk! Yuk! I'm not selling insurance, you loon. I just heard you were getting married, and wanted to make sure you had my address so you can send me an invitation!"

As incredible as it may seem, once the word gets out that you're going to be married, old friends, old enemies, and people you thought were probably dead will crawl out of their holes just to dial your number and ask to be invited to your wedding. What's a groom to do? According to social protocol, it's extremely rude for these clowns to request an invitation. However, many otherwise intelligent people have absolutely no concept of propriety and believe that every wedding is like New Year's Eve in Times Square. When you get a demand like this, do not take the time to define "presumptuousness" to the caller. You're better off being prepared with an answer that the philistine will understand:

"You know, Harvey, it's going to be a smaller wedding than you might think, and we're having trouble just getting both of our families invited. I'm sorry, but we won't be able to invite you."

Whether it's 2:00 A.M. or not, some of the callers won't take no for an answer. They believe that you should be flattered that they want to attend your wedding and can't understand why they shouldn't be invited. Be prepared for a variety of ploys to persuade you that there's got to be room for *just one more* person on the list.

They'll try nostalgia:

"Gosh, remember the time we went to the Clemson game and I got drunk and ripped the urinal off the wall? That was the highlight of my life, and you were there with me, bailing me out," says the caller from the past.

"The good old days," you sigh.

Then you get firm: *"Harvey, we can only invite so many, and I'm afraid the invitations have already gone out."*

They'll attempt to convince you of the depth of their feelings toward you:

"You know, of all the people in the world, you were always there for me. In the back of my mind, I've always thought that, more than anyone else, I wanted to see you get married."

Your reply: *"That's very flattering, Dopslinger. I think a lot of you, too. It was very difficult deciding who we could invite to the wedding, but when the chips came down, we just couldn't get everybody in."*

The cardinal rule is that once you've agonized over creating a guest list you and your bride can live with, stick by it. Just because it's improper for acquaintances to fish for invitations doesn't mean that they won't try it. Saying, "Sure, you can come," may make you feel like a nice guy while you're on the phone, but it's sure to stir up trouble with your fiancée and others involved in planning and paying for the wedding.

Derek, a 27-year-old groom who works in the film industry, came under heavier pressure than most to send out a few extra invitations. It seemed that every acquaintance, co-worker, and ghost from his past perceived his upcoming wedding as a great place to network for jobs, and took it upon themselves to get invited. Because he was unprepared for "phone calls from the dead," he started saying "yes" to a few casual acquaintances, and soon had some run-ins with his bride-to-be, Marla, who was upset at the growing number of names on his list. She told him clearly, "No more guests," and was justified since she was paying.

Derek found himself in a difficult position: He didn't want to upset Marla by inviting any additional friends, and yet he had set a precedent by sending invitations to the first few scroungers who had hinted that they'd like to attend. The pot boiled over when Jack, a close co-worker of Derek's, acted hurt because he hadn't received an invitation even though another colleague, who wasn't particularly close to Derek, had demanded and gotten one.

Derek caved in under the guilt and secretly addressed an envelope to Jack, thinking that he could slip one more person into the wedding without telling Marla about it. While that ploy may have temporarily eased his mind about his co-worker's feelings, he wasn't prepared for the message from Jack that his fiancée overheard on his phone machine, which said, "This is Jack. I wanted to give you my address for the invitation."

Marla hit the roof, since Derek had promised not to invite any more guests. Derek tried to justify his actions by explaining the tale of how the other worker got invited and Jack was closer and blah blah blah, but Marla didn't buy it for a minute. Instead, she chased the postman down the street, begging him to give her back the offending invitation. Postmen are not allowed to give mail to anyone other than the addressee, so she returned home, empty-handed and furious. To save face, Derek had to hide in front of Jack's house, steal the invitation out of his mailbox (a federal crime), and explain to Jack that he wouldn't be invited after all.

Derek and Marla made up and were happily married, but not before she hid the blank invitations at her mother's house and steamed over Derek's faux pas for a day or two. As for Jack, he spontaneously combusted, but that's another story. The moral is never, ever, give in to people who demand seats at your wedding if you don't really want to invite them. If you say yes to those first few who call, you may be starting down a slippery slope toward confrontation. "Just Say No" to people who fish for invitations.

OUT-OF-TOWNER LODGING NIGHTMARE

Ned, a graduate student, married a young woman who had grown up in a town five hundred miles away, where the wedding was to be held. He was able to invite many high school friends and college fraternity brothers to the wedding. Most of them decided to attend, and Ned decided to be a nice guy and make hotel reservations for them.

The whole gang drove convoy-style to the wedding and enjoyed the ceremony and reception immensely. They also liked hotel living for a couple of days and ordered a lot of food and beer from room service. After they'd wished Ned well, they jumped back into their cars and left town, honking and yelling and feeling good about having attended Ned's big day.

When Ned and his new wife went on their honeymoon, they celebrated the first night with a fine meal at a fancy restaurant. Ned gave the waiter his credit card; a few minutes later the maître d' came to Ned's table and told him that he had gone over his limit on his card.

"That's impossible," protested Ned, but the restaurant stood firm. He paid with the little cash they'd brought, and the next day called the credit card company to complain. They told him that two thousand dollars had been billed to his card from the hotel! His buddies had assumed that since he had made the reservations, he would pay for their rooms.

Ned and his wife were forced to shorten their honeymoon, since no hotel or restaurant would honor Ned's credit card. When they returned home, they contacted Ned's friends and persuaded them to pay their hotel bill. It wasn't until a year later that Ned and his wife had the time to take the honeymoon they had originally planned.

Ned's mistake was in assuming that his friends would know to pay their own bills while in town. It seems like an obvious responsibility, but, once again, you run into *people who have seen too many television shows.* On TV, nobody pays for anything. Ned's friends weren't consciously rude—just ignorant and misinformed. He should have told them ahead of time that he would make reservations for them and stated plainly that they were to pay the bill. An even better idea would have been to give them the phone numbers of a couple of hotels, one upscale and one cheap, and let them make their own reservations. That would have kept his name off of any bills.

Another advantage to giving out-of-towners hotel information is that it lets them know ahead of time that they will not be allowed to stay on your couch. Guys like Harvey Dopslinger occasionally go through the following mental process:

"Last year I visited and stayed on his couch. So I'll just

catch a ride to the wedding and crash with the groom. It shouldn't be a problem." If you invite a few out-of-towners, somebody is bound to make that leap of faith. If you invite a lot of out-of-towners, several will assume that they can sleep on your floor. Tell them that while you'd like to have them stay at your place, there are just too many visitors during the wedding to make it practical. If you suspect that some guests are planning to room with you, give them hotel information in a diplomatic way—this lets them know that they'll have to make their own lodging arrangements without implying that they'd be so bass-ackwards as to assume anything else.

DATES

Last year you had a great party and invited many of the pals who will come to your wedding. At last summer's kegger-extravaganza, everyone was welcome to bring a date, and a good time was had by all. It might be nice if all your friends could bring dates to your wedding, but those additional names quickly add up, and either make the wedding more expensive or take up slots you'd rather use to invite people from your "B" and "C" lists.

For your wedding you want to invite only the people specifically named on your lists. An invitation to Harvey Dopslinger means that Harvey is welcome, and Harvey only, unless he is married, in which case his wife must be included in the invitation. A surprising number of nerds don't understand this protocol, as their experience with social events is limited to beer bashes and bowling parties where they were encouraged to bring dates. Your task is to determine which dorks will decide that their sweethearts are welcome, and let them know that's not the case.

Some will blithely confess their intentions, and when they R.S.V.P. they'll announce, "Of course I'll be bringing Heather Marie with me." Just reply, "We are really planning the wedding for only a hundred [or fifty, or whatever] guests. We can't let everybody bring dates, or else we'll soon have twice as many people as we planned."

These bozos may persist as much as the random callers from the past. Again, it's important not to waver. He may say, "But Heather Marie and I have been dating eight and a half weeks, and it's real serious!" Tell him, "There's just not room for even one more person." If he pleads really hard, you can say, "There were people whom I know a lot better than Heather Marie whom I couldn't invite because we only have so much room." If he won't budge, say, "I'm sorry we'll miss you at the wedding." That should give him the hint.

A few invitees won't tell you ahead of time that they're bringing dates, and may just show up at the church with some bimbos from another planet. You can't scrawl across the invitation, "Don't bring a date or you're in trouble," and once these uninvited guests show up, you can't refuse them at the door. You probably know which of your friends might make such a gaffe, and you can launch a preemptive strike by subtly informing them ahead of time that dates are not welcome.

There are a few guests who have justification for bringing an additional person. If a friend or relative is disabled and requires an assistant to push a wheelchair or otherwise aid him, that helper should be included. A separate invitation goes to each member of an engaged couple; if a couple becomes engaged after your invitations are mailed, send a second invitation as soon as possible. Invitations sent to guests who are married should include the name of the spouse; however, if this was overlooked, then mail the forgotten spouse a separate invitation as soon as the error is noticed.

SMALL FRY

Children are another bag o' worms. If you decide that you want guests' progeny at your wedding, put the children's names on the invitations. If you choose not to invite the wee ones, there may still be a bonehead or two out there who decides that his children are invited anyway. As soon as you catch wind of this, let the offending parties know that, as smart and wonderful as their children are, they are to leave them at home. A good way to do this without screaming,

"Don't bring the little monsters!" is to inquire casually, "Have you found a babysitter for the day of the wedding?" They should take the hint, but if they say, "Oh, we were planning on bringing Harvey Junior," then try being more direct, such as, "We'd really appreciate it if you didn't bring your children."

If you and your bride decide to invite children, or if some people bring youngsters along in spite of a request not to, it is important to make arrangements for them. Some churches will allow you to set up a nursery, supervised by a friend, a church worker, or the parents. This way, any babies (invited or uninvited) who attend the ceremony won't disrupt the service.

EX-WIVES, EX-HUSBANDS, EX-LOVERS, AND EX-LIVE-INS

It's the twentieth century, and people's lives are somewhat more complicated than they were in the distant past when the rules of etiquette seem to have been devised. You and your bride may have colorful backgrounds, and one or both of you may have some previous "significant others" who are still close to you. Deciding whether to invite someone who was once a main squeeze can be difficult.

The rule of thumb is not to invite anyone who will detract from the task at hand, which is to marry the bride to the groom. If you have a *Fatal Attraction* girlfriend in your past, don't invite her, as she may scream out obscenities during the ceremony or chase you down the aisle with a carving knife. If it's a level-headed ex-wife with whom you share a child, don't invite her before you discuss the situation with your bride-to-be.

Jeff and Lisa, a couple from Maryland who considered themselves very open-minded, both decided it would be cool to invite several former honeys to their wedding. All of them were very well behaved, except one woman, Elvira (not her real name), who, six years earlier, had lived with Jeff for one semester during college. Elvira (her real name was Sandy D. Elfkin, of Baltimore) got drunk at the reception and told

It's a good idea to think twice before inviting an old girlfriend to your wedding.

WORDING CHOICES AND
BUYING INVITATIONS

Suggestions for wording and purchasing the actual invitations are thoroughly covered in the dozen or so bridal magazines your fiancée has accumulated; in any case, it is a fairly straight-forward proposition. When buying preprinted invitations, the main pitfall lies in the mail-order market. Just like the X-ray specs you ordered as a child, some invitations look better in advertisements than they do in person. Either get a sample invitation from the company or order them from a local printer.

Preprinted invitations can cost as much as two to five dollars apiece, but there are some workable inexpensive alternatives. One solution is to buy blank invitations, and handwrite them, which is officially the "most proper" way to go about it.

gruesome details of her fling with Jeff, before getting into a fistfight with the poor girl who caught the bride's bouquet. Elvira (Sandy Elfkin is now wanted by the FBI on eight counts of criminal emotionality) caused a giant embarrassing ruckus, which might have been avoided if she hadn't been there. Granted, the other ex-lovers might have been excluded also, but in hindsight Jeff and Lisa agreed that that would have been a small price to pay.

With all the bizarre permutations of past live-ins, lovers, and previous "significant others" that can arise, it is tempting to invite them. Remember, though, that they're your past. Your bride is the future. Discuss any potentially difficult guests with your fiancée, and if either of you has reservations, it's probably best to leave them out. As tempting as it is to pretend that the two of you are very hip and above it all, the "ex" list can create uncomfortable situations, no matter how strongly you believe otherwise.

Divorced parents can present another problem. If either of you has parents who have divorced and remarried, the dilemma begins with deciding whom to invite and whom to exclude, and continues when you have to explain your reasoning for doing so. The only hard-and-fast rule is that the bride and groom can ask or exclude anyone they wish, including stepparents, real parents, or anything in between. If you invite both partners of a divorced couple, be sure to notify the ushers that they are to be seated separately, unless they have specifically asked to be together. When you suspect that bringing certain people together will create a fight, bite the bullet and invite only one of them. It's *your* wedding, and anything that will interfere with the event is to be avoided.

5

DIPLOMATIC DEALINGS WITH IN-LAWS: YOUR FAMILY AND HERS

B esides that wonderful gal you're going to marry, you'll be forming relationships with a clan of others whom you may or may not get along with and, more important, who may have serious reservations about you.

Any groom, by the time he's asked a woman to marry him, has been able to get to know his bride, with all her strengths, weaknesses, and quirks. Meeting her family, and introducing her to yours, is another matter entirely.

FAMILIES ARE INSANE

Even if you've met them before, her family's attitude about you will change now that you are around to stay. No longer just "the boyfriend," you are about to become "the son-in-law," "the brother-in-law," and "my niece/sister/granddaughter's husband."

Every family has its own internal rules, logic, and sore spots that are completely irrational and difficult to discern. Your own family is probably somewhat insane. Hers may be no further out to lunch, but because you don't know them, they seem crazier. When you first meet her family as "the fiancé," a good attitude to take is that you are visiting a foreign country where you do not know the lay of the land, and to tread lightly until you discover where the emotional land mines are and know how to avoid them.

In the days of arranged marriages, one of the most important ingredients of a successful union was that the bride's family get along with the groom's family, and if the actual couple getting married despised each other, well, tough luck. At least the possible conflicts were contained to two people. In our enlightened age, the bride and groom select each other, and if the families don't get along, that's where the conflict sets in.

Using massive high-speed computers, it has been demonstrated mathematically that the likelihood of some of your family not liking her, or of her family not liking you, is near certainty, using the following highly scientific formula:

(number of crackpot relatives) × (number of short-tempered relatives) + square root of (stubborness) + (politics) + (religion) + (inflated self-image) × (sports allegiances) = Potential for Conflict

No matter how much she protests otherwise, when you say "I do" to her, you also will marry her whole family. And she will marry yours. Don't break off the engagement over this, however. Dealing with her family is fully survivable if you have an adequate strategy prepared ahead of time.

The goals of pursuing a relationship with your in-laws are as follows:

1. Begin by making a good impression.
2. After you botch that, try to keep from creating a bad impression.
3. Once you've made a bad impression, try to contain damages.
4. When you reach the point where they've decided you're a good-for-nothing, fresh-mouthed, unemployable lunk who duped their sweet daughter into marriage, just don't go near them when they're cleaning their gun collection.

Conflict with your in-laws is inevitable. Your job as a groom is to preserve your relationship with your fiancée, and that will be the cardinal rule of all dealings with your in-laws.

You're going to be semirelated to them for the rest of your life, so it's worthwhile to try to make the best of it while you can.

Just remember, when dealing with your in-laws you merely have to get along with them. You don't have to like them or agree with them.

BEING YOURSELF—DON'T DO IT

Some ill-advised fellow in the past came up with the notion that people should "just be themselves" and not worry about what others think. This may work in college sit-ins, group therapy, and parts of California, but when visiting your in-laws, no course of action could be more foolish or dangerous.

It's pretty important for your well-being and your bride's that you try to get along with your in-laws. If you are overly proud, then swallow your pride and keep quiet about controversial topics. That first meeting is the time, as Mrs. Ward Cleaver liked to say, to "be on your best behavior."

"Best behavior" doesn't mean pretending you're some kind of Medal of Honor winner with Albert Einstein's brain and Clint Eastwood's guts. You've got to appear better than that. *You're taking away their daughter.* As attached as you've grown to her, they've known her longer.

"Best behavior" entails avoiding certain topics of conversation. Among them are:

POLITICS

Political leanings sometimes skip generations, and thus it is likely that although you and your bride may have similar attitudes, you may still be at odds with her parents and yours. There is a family in Phoenix, Arizona, who exemplifies this extremely well. The grandparents of the Price family (not their real name) were political radicals during the 1930s, and they advocated communism in America. As the Depression ended, their beliefs moderated somewhat, but they were still on the far left of the political spectrum.

The Prices' children, born in the late thirties, grew up as

children of privilege, the result of the father's financial success. As they hit adulthood the Price sons discovered political conservatism with a vengeance, and were some of the pillars of Phoenix right-wing society, ready to outlaw liberalism in America and to nuke Russia at a moment's notice.

The grandchildren grew up in the sixties. Far from being right-wing like their parents, instead they became dyed-in-the-wool hippies, occupying buildings, organizing protest marches, and printing underground newspapers. They are still active in Phoenix left-wing politics today.

The point is that all three generations of the Price family, with their clashing political tendencies, still get along extremely well with one another. They get together for dinners, family reunions, and Phoenix Suns' games, and actually enjoy one another's company. Their secret is that although all three generations are sincerely committed to different political beliefs, they find lots of other common ground on which they can agree. They all realize there's more to life than politics.

Your family may be Democrats and hers Republicans. You may hate the incumbent, and her mother might have campaigned for him. One important lesson of marriage is that people whose politics differ from yours are not necessarily evil, twisted perverts who want to sell America to the Russians. Do not bring up politics the first eight hundred or so times you visit your new family. This may seem like a cop-out or a wimpy course of action, but there is an inverse ratio between your political passion and the amount of time you should spend talking about it with her family—in other words, the more certain you are that you are right, the more urgent the requirement that you should shut up about it.

There are plenty of other safe subjects for human discourse, from barbecue recipes to that great team, the [_insert local team of choice here_]. _Anything_ is better than politics, but if you're truly motivated to push your cause, push it on strangers and people at the office before you visit your in-laws. Go knock on some doors, start a petition, write a letter to the editor, just do something to get it out of your system before you visit your new relatives, and you'll be on much surer footing.

If the Prices can put away political differences in order to preserve family relationships, anybody can, and chances are you don't differ as violently with your in-laws as you may think. Now, if *they* should bring up politics (and they will), you may feel as if they drew first blood and that therefore you're free to go for the jugular. Far from it. Think about some reasonable conversational dodges that you can use as answers, ones that are not inflammatory but don't make you sound like a wimp.

Try laughing and saying, "Hah! Politics—who can ever figure it out?" If they persist, say, "I don't really want to get into politics right now." If they persist after a direct refusal like that, try some conversational diversionary tactics, like, "How about some more of that delicious pie?" or, "That's a lovely pin you're wearing, Mrs. Cleaver."

When someone demands that you take a political stand, he or she may be picking a fight, and it's a good opportunity to use some conversational jujitsu to turn the question around. Try, "I'd really be interested in hearing *your* opinion of the president, Mr. Cleaver." This almost always works, because those who pick political fights usually are more interested in talking than in listening. After asking for an opinion, listen, smile, nod, and say noncommittal but pseudothoughtful things like, "How interesting," and, "I see what you're saying."

Caution: The inverse law of political passion matters most at a juncture like this. The stronger your disagreement with a future in-law's political opinion, the more important it is that you shut up. If you think your future father-in-law is a blithering, dangerous radical, **it doesn't matter,** because *it's more important that you get along with him than that you agree with him.* Just nod and smile as long as necessary, then ask for another piece of pie.

RELIGION: SHUT THY MOUTH

Most of the really violent wars being fought in the world today are waged in part over religious differences. There is a good likelihood that your religious beliefs and those of your in-laws will differ. Even if you're in the same church, they may disagree with your opinions about it, and although it's not likely that they'll try to start a war with you, be mindful that religious convictions run deep.

This may seem like sacrilege to some folks, but all belief systems have some version of "Honor thy father and mother," and this applies to father-in-law and mother-in-law also. "Honor," in this context, means "Shut thy mouth."

PERSONAL FAILINGS

Face it, you've had some personal failures, everybody has. George Washington cut down his parents' cherry tree. Thoreau spent a couple of nights in jail for not paying his taxes. Even Lee Iacocca had to take a government handout. Everybody has a "past."

Did you fail a class? Get a drunk-driving citation? Lose a job? Tear the tags off a mattress? Shred hundreds of top-secret government documents at the Pentagon? Or maybe, during a crime spree that lasted an entire Red Sox season, you video-taped games without the express written consent of the commissioner of baseball. Whatever your failing, if your in-laws don't need to know, don't bring it up. Some people have a strong confessional urge, and believe (wrongly) that spilling all the bad beans from their ugly pasts will make them appear honest and human. It doesn't. It only makes them appear bad.

The stronger your urge to confess a personal failure, the more important it is that you *shut up*. You'll do plenty of foolish and stupid things in the future, which you'll have to answer for, and some of your past failings will be discovered anyway, so there is no reason to let them know every detail of your life at this point. These are your in-laws, not your therapist or priest.

Occasionally you'll be cornered on a point of past history that you'd rather not discuss. At times like that, it's a good idea to admit you were wrong, learned from the experience, and won't stray that way again. Mr. Cleaver may bear down on you at a Thanksgiving visit and say, "You used to work for my golf partner, and he told me that you killed all the chickens in the hen house by leaving the heater on in the summer." If it's true, say, "Yes, that's true, and I feel terrible about it. But I was younger then, and I learned *an important lesson* about chickens, heat, and weather." Bad answers include: "Yes, I meant to do it," "Your golf partner is the lamest jerk I ever met in my life," and, "I hate chickens—I'm *glad* they died, and I'd do it again if I had the chance."

ESTABLISHING INDEPENDENCE
(Without Getting Disinherited)

Putting on the dog and pony show when you visit your in-laws is barely tolerable for short periods of time. Most guys are happy to be sociable when necessary, but then they want to be left alone (with their fiancées/wives) to do their own thing. The crisis comes when in-laws start invading your new life, and want to tell you what to do, where to work, how to dress, how to decorate your apartment, what kind of car to drive, and which newspaper to read.

During the months before a wedding, and in the first year of marriage, it's vital that you and your wife demonstrate clearly that you're going to make your own decisions and pursue your own course in life.

Whether they live across the street or across the continent, her parents (and yours) will try to put their stamp on you and your wife. Your parents and your in-laws have only the best of intentions: they believe they know what's good for you.

The younger you and your wife are, the more they will want to "help" you. The most innocent actions can become the most invasive, and it's important that you be prepared to refuse unwanted intrusions. If you're living in their home, the pressure can be even worse.

Wayne and Vicki lived together before getting married, and both worked long hours. The week of the bridal shower, Vicki had no time to clean up her apartment, so she recruited her mother to help.

Wayne too was grateful for the help that week, and the place looked perfect for the shower. Well, Vicki's mother kept the key, and started coming over while they were at work, just to do a little "tidying up" from time to time. This eventually grew into making them dinner a couple of times a week, unasked, and soon it happened more often than not that Vicki's mother was there cooking when Wayne got home from work.

This mother-in-law was always apologizing for being there, but she *was* there. She often asked, "If you don't want me to stay, I'll go, I won't mind a bit," but neither Wayne nor Vicki had the heart to say, "Okay, take a hike, babe," since she was being so "nice."

When Wayne and Vicki got back from their honeymoon, the whole place had been deep-cleaned within an inch of its life, and there were new, strange pictures on the wall— Norman Rockwell prints and crying clowns. Wayne and Vicki's rock-and-roll posters were nowhere to be seen. Streamers and signs were hung up that said WELCOME BACK NEWLYWEDS, and in the middle of all the alien decoration, humming along to the mellow sounds of *A Very Special Night with Engelbert Humperdink,* was Vicki's mother, who shrieked, "I just couldn't wait to see the happy couple!"

Wayne blew up real good. It was the crying clown pictures that put him over the brink, but sometimes it takes extremes to make a man realize what he must do. He told her, "Please leave. We'll call you. Just please leave." Vicki's mother quite sheepishly picked up her things and left, apologizing the whole way out.

Shortly after putting the clowns into the back of the closet and stashing Engelbert under the couch, Wayne and Vicki had a talk about setting some rules for visits. No uninvited cleaning. No unasked-for dinners. Above all, Vicki's mother had to call before visiting. Their apartment was much messier after that, but they kept their sanity.

It's not always pathological thoughtfulness that creates a problem. Control is the real issue. When in-laws (or your parents) begin to nose into your life in such a way that it creates a problem, it's crucial to recognize the pattern and nip it in the bud before it becomes habit.

You and your fiancée should begin making independent decisions *before* saying "I do," to create a precedent. A good decision to begin with is the choice of a place to live. If your in-laws want to make suggestions, listen to them carefully, but you and your fiancée should then make the choice on your own.

Also, set some rules about the nature and extent of the input both of your families can have in your lives. Without appearing rude or oversensitive, it is possible to set down some rules. Rules that everyone in the universe *except* in-laws seems to follow instinctively. Like:

1. Don't come over without calling first.
2. Don't call three times a day asking if you can come over.
3. Don't schedule our free time for us ("I wanted you to come over for brunch on Saturday and then Sunday I thought we could all go to one of those Benji movies").

Some common problems in establishing independence include:

1. *Holidays.* Both families believe that the two of you should come to *their* homes. There are several solutions to this. Either alternate families (e.g., hers in odd years, your in even years), alternate holidays (e.g., her family gets Thanksgiving, you family gets Christmas or Chanukah every year), or start your own traditions. Holidays are stressful anyway, and it is inevitable that you will be breaking someone's tradition. If both families are in town, you may be tempted to try "double duty," hitting both families at every holiday every year, but this can turn what should be fun occasions into Type A marathons of overeating and split-second scheduling. Try to create a workable solution in advance, so that no one is disappointed. A month or so before a holiday, call your parents (or hers) and tell them that you're planning to visit the other family this year. If you wait till Thanksgiving Day to decide, one family will be angry that you're late and the other disappointed that you have to leave so soon. And you'll be chugging down the Alka-Seltzer.

At holidays, remember that you and your wife are now a viable family unit of your own and should call your own shots.

2. *Out-of-town relatives (hers or yours) who want you to move to where they are.* If you don't want to move, stress the reasons why you're happy where you are: "We like living here. I have a job and friends here, and so does she."

3. *Meddlesome second-guessing that comes in the guise of helpfulness.* Mother-in-law: "I just thought you might be tired of wearing those blue jeans all the time, so I got you eight pairs of stretch plaid polyester slacks. And I know a really good barber who can straighten up whatever happened there

THE IN-LAW GUIDE TO APPEARANCES AND REALITY

If you try to appear	Your in-laws will think you are
Thoughtful and quiet	Uptight and shy
The life of the party	Overbearing, obnoxious, and rude
Casual	An unrepentant slob
Sophisticated	A snob
Intelligent	A know-it-all
Sober	A teetotaler
Hardworking	A workaholic who will leave their daughter alone on weekends
A guy who likes to spend time with family	Unemployed
Well dressed	Vain
Funny	Goofy
Sociable	A party animal
Cautious	Paranoid

on your head. And Elroy offered to sponsor you for membership in the Loyal Order of the Water Buffalo—they don't let just anyone in, you know, and it'll give you something to do with your Thursdays and most weekends. The swearing-in ceremony is this week and you really should go." When these kinds of offers are put forth, you may feel obliged to accept, no matter how contrary to your very nature they seem. Chances are your wife/fiancée will experience the same sorts of offers from your family and has created a strategy to deal with them.

SO YOU'VE OFFENDED AN IN-LAW: HOW TO CONTAIN DAMAGES

You did your best. You didn't talk about politics, religion, or that time you got drunk and got a mohawk. You've stayed up late at night on numerous occasions cleaning your little homestead before they came for a visit. You even let her father smoke his cheap cigars in your den without so much as a cough. And yet . . . it happened. You did the inevitable. You have entered the faux pas zone.

Darius, who works in an engine reboring shop in Kentucky, thought he had a pretty good relationship with his fiancée's parents, whom he'd met twice. Several weeks before the wedding, he was visiting her family (who lived in Cincinnati) at a Fourth of July barbecue. Mr. Paplaczyk (Darius's future father-in-law) realized that they needed more barbecue sauce before they could start cooking. Darius volunteered to drive, but Mr. Paplaczyk insisted on driving, and Darius went along for the ride. Two blocks from home, Mr. Paplaczyk took a chance on a yellow light, and lost. He was hit by a lady coming home from church.

No one was hurt, but at this point Mr. Paplaczyk, who had knocked back a few beers at the party, asked Darius to pretend *he* had been driving, for the police and the insurance company. Darius refused, since his job involved driving a company truck, and he couldn't afford to have the ticket on his record.

Even though Mr. Paplaczyk was found to be under the limit as far as the beers were concerned, from that day on his future in-laws considered Darius an uptight moralist who blew a chance to help out a family member in need.

Darius felt he was in the right, and he was. But from the Fourth of July on, his in-laws never really liked him as much as they had at first. Darius expected Mr. Paplaczyk to come to his senses and say he was sorry to have asked Darius to compromise himself. The Paplaczyks wanted Darius to apologize for being so unhelpful.

What's a guy to do? If they had been anyone in the world except for his fiancée's family, he would have simply blown them off and never visited again. However, Sonja, his fiancée, was pretty close to her family, so that wasn't an option.

You probably won't be put in Darius's situation, but eventually you will forget a birthday, unwittingly insult a family friend, break an heirloom, drink too much, be seen wearing your KILL 'EM ALL—LET GOD SORT 'EM OUT T-shirt, drop a case of 10W-40 on their rug, or in some other manner find yourself on the wrong side of your in-laws, *no matter how hard you try otherwise.* No one can (or should) always be on his best behavior, and, as they say in the construction industry, "things happen."

The cardinal rule in dealings with in-laws is considering the question, "How does this affect my relationship with my fiancée (and later, my wife)?" Darius was a stubborn guy and wasn't about to get on his knees and apologize, but he was bothered by all the grief the Paplaczyks were inflicting on Sonja. If her mother called, and he answered the phone, she'd just say, "Tell Sonja to call home," then hang up.

Two weeks before the wedding, he knew he had to do something. He asked Sonja how he might bury the hatchet with his future father-in-law. Darius found out that Mr. Paplaczyk was a big Mets fan, and decided that he would not apologize for or even talk about the unfortunate Fourth of July run-in, but instead just got tickets to the Reds-Mets game that week and invited Mr. Paplaczyk, who accepted. Darius drove.

They never resolved the fight over the accident explicitly, but by taking the old man to a ball game, Darius was able to normalize the situation, and Sonja's family started talking to him again when he answered the phone.

"That won't work," you say. "My father-in-law *hates* the Mets!" The point is not that the Mets are the answer to all your problems, but rather that some conflicts are unresolvable. Dwelling on a particular fight, or problem, is rarely the answer. Sometimes it just takes finding some common ground and exploring it, realizing that certain conflicts will never be won or lost.

You will not be able to resolve every problem with your in-laws. Sometimes, people have to agree to disagree.

6

THE
GIFT LIST

If you don't let people know what you might like as a wedding gift, you will be buried under a mountain of toaster ovens.

How many china patterns can you name? Fifty? Okay, how about two? None?

*F*act: Many of the people invited to your wedding will feel socially obligated to give an appropriate wedding gift to you and your new wife.

Fact: If you do not let people know what you might like as a wedding gift, you will receive enough toaster ovens to open a chain of restaurants called "Cheese Toast Hut."

Fact: To the naïve groom it may seem somewhat greedy to tell people what he and his wife want. "It's up to them if they want to get us something," believes this open-minded soul. "I don't want to *tell* them."

Fact: Anyone who is kind enough to send a gift to you and your fiancée is hoping to find something that you'll like and use and don't already have. The truth of the matter is, *they don't want to get you a toaster oven if someone else already has.* But if you do not, somehow, let people know what you want and need, they will innocently buy what seems like a good, practical gift—for example, a toaster oven. (*Opening Soon—Cheese Toast Hut!*)

Solution: As you may have already heard from your fiancée, there is a road out from the mountain of toaster ovens. There is a perfectly legitimate social institution developed specifically to help thoughtful gift-givers find things that the new couple wants. It's called the gift registry, and there are several popular variations on this age-old method of leaking the inside dope on what you and your wife-to-be want in your home.

CREATING A GIFT LIST

It's several months before the wedding, and you suspect that someone, somewhere, might buy you a wedding gift if you invite him to your wedding. The time has come to have a powwow with your fiancée to determine what kind of objects you want to surround yourself with once you've tied the knot.

As in any negotiation, there is a hidden agenda. It's not good enough to decide, "We need plates, sheets, cups, and some cooking utensils." For example, take plates. An innocent enough household item. Are they going to be white plates, plates covered with flowers, incredibly hip ultramodern plates covered with triangles, squares, and circles? Are they to be Batman plates (your personal favorite)? As they say in those newspapers at the grocery checkout, "The kind of stuff you own reveals your personality."

Your typical American male ambles along in life, always looking at the food, never at the plate, unless it's really dirty or something. Then one day he gets engaged, and his fiancée asks him, "What kind of china should we get?" For one thing, most guys never even use the term *china*. (In the locker room, after the football game, how often have you heard the quarterback say, "Hey Frank! Didja see the new china patterns?" Okay, maybe once or twice when Rosie Greer still played.)

Forced to make a decision of some sort on this subject, the groom can either (a) smile and say, "Whatever you want, honey," (b) panic, look at hundreds of china patterns, pick one arbitrarily, and argue with his fiancée until she agrees or he gives up, or (c) thoughtfully consider all the patterns, consult with his fiancée, and decide on one that they both like.

HOW MUCH INPUT SHOULD THE GROOM HAVE? (How Much Do You Care?)

"C," the "mutual consent" option, probably never happens naturally, but your fiancée would be thrilled if it *appeared* that you two had happily agreed on a gift list. Before you sit down with your fiancée, look at a gift-list form in one of the bridal magazines. Scratch out all the things about which you've never had a strong opinion one way or another. Is there anything remaining that's not scratched out? If not, it wouldn't be unusual.

If for some reason you really do love china and silver and linen patterns and know all about them, *more power to you.* You probably would relish the chance to hash out a gift registry with your fiancée and will enjoy every minute. If, however, you'd just as soon eat off a plate bearing a picture of the Caped Crusader, it's important to make your fiancée believe that you *really do care* about this important life decision.

To accomplish this, sit down with your fiancée and contemplate each item you wish to have in your new household— crystal, china, linens, et cetera. She may by this time have armed herself with a huge stack of "informational brochures" (some would call them advertisements) that the manufacturers have sent. Look through them *thoughtfully* (in other words, alternately nod, say "hmmm," and shake your head), then pick one. Any pattern will do—unless you genuinely have a favorite, *unless you really care about china.* She'll have picked a different pattern from the one you selected. Look again at the brochures, even more thoughtfully (all of the above business, plus gritting your teeth), and open to her choice of pattern. Say, "You know, I think I like this one better, Sheila,"* pointing to the one she favored. Then extol the virtues of that particular pattern; i.e., "I really like the thin line around the edge," or whatever.

There are two reasons to go through this little bit of playacting. First, it reassures your fiancée that she's done a good job of executing this prenuptial task. Although women are much more likely to understand the important difference between having spring roses and winter roses on their dish towels, it is

---

*If your wife is not named Sheila, use her own name, or you could be in for real trouble.

very probable that this is the first time your fiancée has had to make a judgment of this sort, and she may suffer from troubling doubts about the correctness of her taste. Your input will help her feel she's done the right thing, so she can finalize the decision and quit losing sleep over the subject. Then she can get on to the *really* important things like deciding between cheese blintzes and chicken petit fours for the reception.

Second, the advantage of pretending to be concerned over the "you pick it, honey" attitude is that it cements in your fiancée's mind what a good catch you are. A man who cares about crystal, china, and linens is a righteous family man and the kind of guy a girl wants to marry. She'll be reminded once again what a first-class domestic dude you'll be (and you are, too). Don't let anyone tell you otherwise. And don't let on if you merely look at the food, not the plate. [Author's note to his own wife if she ever reads this: Unlike the mock concern advocated here, *I really truly believe housewares are a very important part of our life together. Seriously.*]

There is one more thing that you and your fiancée should do in preparing your gift list, and that is to include a variety of items in a variety of price ranges. There are all kinds of things you may need beyond crystal, china, and linen, and it is extremely thoughtful to include some inexpensive gift items. It is the *thought* that counts, not the price, and chances are a couple of years ago you never would have considered dropping a hundred bucks on a wedding gift for a friend.

REGISTERING VERSUS "INFORMAL" GIFT LISTS

The very act of preparing a gift list may seem a little self-centered, and can make a groom feel like some sort of terrorist making up his list of demands. Even on your birthday you would never consider calling people and telling them exactly what you want, but that's not what you'll be doing. Many department and specialty stores offer what seems a marvelous service—bridal registry.

THANK-YOU NOTES

Every gift given to you and your bride has to be acknowl-edged with a *handwritten thank-you note*. A phone call will not cut the mustard, and writing a computer program that randomly generates warm sentiments is also out of the ques-tion. Although traditionally it is the bride who writes thank-you notes, remember that the tradition originated in a time when no women worked, the Dodgers were still in Brooklyn, people had lots of free time, and marriages were as often as not arranged by parents.

Things have changed. You will be enjoying the gifts as much as your fiancée will, so it is only fair that you should offer to write your share of the thank-yous. If she declines your offer and decides to write them all herself, you can at least help by keeping track of who gave you what and when they were thanked. But if you do end up writing thank-you notes, remember that they must be sincere and specific:

Dear Kind Relative: Thank you for the lovely gift. We really like it a lot. Sincerely, Doug, will not do. Although the letter does not have to be long, it must (1) specifically name the gift, (2) specifically name the giver, and (3) offer a sentence or two about how it will fit into your new life. The note above would be much stronger if he had written: *Dear Aunt Sharon: Thank you so much for the beautiful place setting. It will make having guests over a lot more fun now that we no longer have to serve them off of our Batman plates! Yours was actually the first place setting we have received, and Alison kept taking it out of the box just to look at. Again, thank you very much. Love, Doug.*

When people go to the trouble to find a gift that you want, wrap it, and ship it to you, the minimum courtesy is to write them. It also lets them know that what they ordered is what you got—sometimes, stores will ship the wrong merchandise, and there is no way of finding out such an error unless the purchaser knows what was received.

A bridal registry is a handwritten or computerized list, prepared by the groom and bride (and her mother and whoever else noses in), and given to a store that will keep track of what has been purchased and what hasn't. For instance, if you register for a china pattern, a silverware pattern, and a variety of other goodies, when the first gift giver to go to that store checks in with the registry, the shop clerk will help him or her select a toaster oven. Then, each subsequent gift giver will be informed, "They've already gotten a toaster oven. How about dish towels?"

These kind shop clerks will ensure that there is no duplication of gifts and will help the gift givers find something that you genuinely need. Once someone purchases a gift, they mark down what has been purchased, and they keep everything up to date.

No matter where you register your gift list, there is still one remaining question: Who distributes this information? Isn't it uncool to call everyone up and say, "Go over to Wayne and Grayson and buy us something nice?" The answer is that invited guests will generally call the parents, or the family member they know best, and ask. Or they may even call you or your bride. If you're asked, just reply, "We're registered at Wayne and Grayson." If you have an individual handling the duties, you can tell them, "Call up Aunt Sally. She's keeping track of things."

INEXPENSIVE GIFTS YOU MAY REALLY NEED

Carrot peeler	Spice set
Apple cutter	Paper
Towel rack	Pens/Pencils
Coffee filters	Soap dish
Coffee mugs	Shower caddy
Strainer	Games/Cards
Cookie sheets	Door mats
Screwdrivers, hammers, nails, etc.	Photo albums
	Weird kitchen utensils

Can opener

Thermos

Funnel

Cake pans

Pointy steel needle thing that goes in the bottom of a flower vase

Magazine rack

Pillows

Flower vases

Spice racks

Jell-O molds that make little Jell-O creatures

Washcloths

Knife sharpeners

Cookbooks

Batteries

Light bulbs

Christmas decorations

Picture frames

SMARTNESS BOX:
Know Your Gifts

Even if you don't care about the difference between royal blue and navy blue you can still participate in the gift-registration process by appearing to be an expert on crystal, silver, and china. There are lots of cryptic terms found in bridal magazines and catalogs, and most are never explained. Following are some definitions to make you a smart groom:

Fine silver is 99.9 percent pure silver. Chemists know it as Ag, but pure silver is too soft to make good dinnerware.

Sterling silver is an alloy of 92.5 percent silver and 7.5 percent copper.

Electroplating is a process by which a thin coat of silver is deposited on a less expensive metal. The metal underneath is usually an alloy of nickle, copper, and zinc.

Glass is made from silica (sand) and potash or soda. It was invented by the Egyptians in the fifteenth century B.C.

Crystal is glass that contains a high percentage of lead oxide in addition to the sand and potash, and is also called leaded glass. *Half-lead* crystal has 24 percent lead oxide, and *full-lead* has 30 percent lead oxide.

Cut glass has designs cut into it by a spinning wheel of iron or stone.

Pressed glass may look like cut glass but is usually cheaper. There is often a seam where the mold halves were joined, unlike true cut glass, which is seamless.

Glassblowing was invented in Rome in the first century.

Bone china really does contain bones. Mixed in with the porcelain (paste) is the ash of calcined bones, which makes a harder, more valuable dish.

Pewter is 91 percent tin, 7 percent antimony, and 2 percent copper. Antique pewter may contain lead, but no lead is allowed in modern pewter (lead can poison the user).

Brass is made of copper and zinc.

Cheese toast is a tasty snack made in a toaster oven by melting pieces of cheese onto slices of bread.

7

RABBIS,
PRIESTS, AND
MINISTERS

YOUR CLERGYMAN: THE MISSION SPECIALIST?

W ho has married a thousand women, yet still remains single?" A priest, of course. When it gets down to the practical details of a religious ceremony, no one knows better than your rabbi, priest, or minister. When the time comes, most religious organizations have either a prayer book or a leaflet describing the way it is usually done. If you have any questions about the procedure of the ceremony or the words that are used, ask the officiant. He or she will be glad to provide an answer and can usually provide valuable insight.

Too many options can become overwhelming. Picking a dress, planning a reception, and deciding what kind of cake, food, and drink to serve, are all left up to you and (mostly) your bride to decide. A religious wedding provides an immovable object around which to put the unstoppable force of the secular elements of the wedding.

Contact the person whom you'd like to officiate at your marriage as soon as possible after you become engaged. If, like so many, you desire to be married on a Saturday in June, remember, there are only four Saturdays in that month, and the availability of the church or temple may dictate the date of your wedding. Some overly optimistic couples have gone as far as announcing a date, only to find that they have to change it when they discover another couple has beaten them to the spot.

Every faith, and every individual clergyman, has rules about what can and cannot be done. Some officiants refuse to perform marriages outside the church or temple proper; others have restrictions as to which days of the week weddings can take place. In the first meeting with your prospective officiant, listen and ask questions so that you leave knowing at least the following:

1. What premarital counseling is required?
2. What days are the officiant and the place we'd like to be married available?
3. What costs will we be asked to pay? (Consider any "suggested donation" as a real, hard cost; refusing to pay it is rude and inconsiderate.) Who pays the musicians?
4. Can we choose our own music?
5. Can we change the words of the ceremony?
6. Will there be a sermon? Can we suggest a topic?
7. If you and your fiancée are of different faiths, can clergymen from both faiths officiate at the marriage jointly?
8. Are there any rules about the religion of your attendants? the guests at the wedding?

Chances are, your clergyman will fill you in on most of the details right away, but if something is not mentioned, be certain to ask. It would be a bad ninth-inning choke to discover at the rehearsal that your best man was barred from participating in the ceremony because he is of a different religion. Be certain to ask.

At that first meeting with your clergyman, don't ask too *many* questions, either. Decisions about who stands where and the proper order for guests to enter can be decided at the rehearsal. Your main goal at the first meeting is to find out what has to happen before the wedding, and to uncover any potential problems while there is still an opportunity to do something about them.

COUNSELING

Robb, a college student just about to graduate, was to marry his girlfriend of many years, Elisa. Like the majority of couples marrying today, they agreed that a church wedding would be nice. The actual act of approaching the officials at his church scared Robb, however. In the four years since high school, he had attended church only three times, at Christmas, and now he had to approach the minister to see if he could be married there.

Robb was embarrassed by his poor attendance and felt somewhat guilty asking his minister to perform his wedding. When he got up the guts to make the visit, he was surprised at two things: first, his minister welcomed his request and didn't even mention Robb's spotty attendance; second, his minister took a much greater interest in his life and marriage than just agreeing to perform a ceremony.

Robb had expected a lecture. His situation is extremely common, however, and most clergymen see a wedding as an opportunity to win back followers to the flock. Rather than make the prospective groom feel guilty, a rabbi, priest, or minister will more often see the desire for a church wedding as a renewed commitment. Don't be surprised if the subject of *future* church membership comes up during the discussion of your wedding.

The bigger surprise often comes when a prospective groom discovers that the clergy often look beyond the mere wedding to help ensure that the couple has a successful marriage. Many churches require counseling before performing a wedding ceremony, and some even offer weekend retreats where couples about to be married can discuss all the "hard" questions they have been avoiding.

Then the minister said the words that scared Robb down to the bottom of his heart: "We require that you and your fiancée come in for four sessions of premarital counseling with me." *Premarital counseling?* he thought. *I never heard about that. Let's just do it Old West style, and I'll pay the preacherman fifty bucks to solemnize the union, and that's that.* Of course he didn't verbalize those thoughts. He just said, "Um, okay, how about next week?"

The role of the clergy in weddings has changed significantly since the Old West days, and they are more interested in the marriage than the wedding. With everyone else around you concentrating on the wedding itself rather than the marriage (*Shall we have petit fours or cucumber sandwiches?*), it can be shocking and refreshing to discover someone who keeps an eye on the bigger picture.

Robb lost some sleep worrying about what would happen in the counseling sessions. Although his was a rather middle-of-the-road congregation, free of the fire-and-brimstone stuff, he imagined that the minister would lay down plenty of difficult, unworkable rules for his married life, and that he'd fidget uncomfortably and have to agree to demands he knew he'd never follow. *"No drinking, no dancing, no laughter at inappropriate jokes, and go to church every Sunday once you're married,"* he imagined the minister bellowing at him and Elisa. *"Don't ever go into debt, and start having children immediately!"*

On the contrary, he found that the counseling was filled with practical, down-to-earth advice, and the minister brought up many important issues that he and Elisa had either been avoiding or hadn't thought of. What are your opinions about how to spend your time? Your money? What do you see yourself doing in five years? Ten years? How do *you* feel about children? Since Elisa works, how are you going to do the housework? What kind of arguments do you have? How do you resolve them?

Rather than dictate to them about how to lead a righteous life, the minister just asked a lot of questions and got the two to talk about the important issues. They found that their minister wasn't just helping them plan the event of the wedding, he was trying to get them to think about their life as a married couple. After leaving the first counseling session, Robb and Elisa stayed up late talking about a whole range of subjects that they felt were important. His fear of clergy was quickly replaced by a feeling that here was one sane person out of the whole gang of people involved with the wedding—someone who was looking at the bigger picture.

What If They Ask Us to Go to a Weekend Seminar?

Some faiths suggest or require that a couple attend a weekend seminar, such as Engaged Encounter, sometime before the ceremony. It you're like most, giving up two whole days of football games and movies may seem a high price to pay just to get married, but those who have attended report only favorable comments about such sessions.

Engaged Encounter is a spin-off of Marriage Encounter, a program imported to the United States from Spain in the 1960s. The weekend seminar, originally developed for Catholics, has transcended its roots and is now offered by a variety of faiths, including Jewish and others. It's not two days of Bible beating and singing hymns; rather, the focus is on helping couples develop strong communication skills, with the ultimate aim of making their future marriage a stronger partnership.

Although the activities vary as decided by individual group leaders, at all of the seminars you can expect to do a variety of exercises aimed at teaching you and your fiancée more about each other, and helping you develop skills that will enable you to interact in a more positive way. According to the National Coordinator of Catholic Engaged Encounter, topics that are always covered include marriage morality, becoming a family, signs of a closed relationship, decisions in marriage, and sex and sexuality.

SHE'S A DIFFERENT RELIGION: WILL WE BOTH BURN IN HELL, OR WHAT?

In the Columbus, Ohio, *Yellow Pages*, under the heading "Churches," there are more than a thousand organizations listed. Columbus is not unusual; in the town live fewer than a million people, which works out to better than one church for every one thousand people. With so many different faiths, it's not unusual for your fiancée to belong to a different one from yours, which in paradise should not be a problem but often is in the real world.

Some religious groups will not perform interfaith marriages at all, others will allow them only if the outsider converts, and still others see no conflict in marrying any two people who genuinely love each other, regardless of their religious beliefs. If there is going to be a problem, you'll probably find it out the first time you approach your clergyman.

Merely ignoring the question and opting for a civil ceremony is a quick and easy answer, but if you or your fiancée have sincerely held beliefs, it merely delays the crisis till a later date. Deciding how children should be raised should not be put off till they're in diapers, and the conflict of how to celebrate religious holidays is best discussed before they're here.

You won't (necessarily) burn in hell, but your time here on earth may be a little hotter. Don't let religious differences become a wedge that splits the two of you apart. Take the initiative, discuss the subject with your fiancée, and decide what action to take. There are plenty of happily married couples who worship differently and keep separate faiths during the whole course of their lives. Just don't ignore the subject, hoping it will go away. It won't.

On the day of the wedding, remember that it is *your* responsibility as groom to pay the officiant. You can use your best man as an intermediary, but "forgetting" to pay is a clumsy and foolish act that can only make you look bad in the eyes of everyone. Chances are, the bride's family is picking up the lion's share of the bills, so paying the clergyman gives the groom an opportunity to participate. More important, it's a powerful symbolic gesture. Your paying the clergyman is an indication that you want to get married. Make sure to give at least the "minimum donation," and possibly even more. It will be the first financial transaction you execute as a married man, so don't botch it.

8

THE LAW

hy should the groom waste time thinking about the law during the hectic period before the wedding? The unprepared groom assumes that marriage is all about true love, the commitment between himself and his fiancée, and perhaps finding a nice suit. However, "just between me and my girl" is a sentiment best reserved for the indecisive couples who choose to live together forever out of wedlock. Tying the knot brings a third party into the relationship—the state.

Marriage is an arrangement between a man, a woman, and the state. The moment your fiancée becomes your wife, your legal status changes significantly, and it pays to learn about the manifestations of that change. You should know what kinds of questions to ask, where to look for answers, and what action to take to protect you and your spouse from potential pitfalls.

LEGAL ADVANTAGES

Married couples enjoy a wealth of legal benefits that mere persons-of-the-opposite-sex-sharing-living-quarters (what lawyers call POSSLQs, the legal way of saying "couples who live together unmarried") cannot always enjoy. Although "just living together" is *tolerated,* it is not *protected legally* as thoroughly as marriage is.

Take the case of Ernie and Theresa, who choose to "just live together" in a state that will remain unnamed but that we'll call Potato and spend all the money that would have gone into their wedding on a good set of power tools and an encyclopedia. On day one of their cohabitation, Ernie sets up the band saw to make an oak rack for the encyclopedia, slips, and saws off his right hand. He falls to the ground, unconscious.

Theresa speeds Ernie to the hospital. The doctors ask Theresa who can legally authorize surgery. Ernie's legal next of kin is his father, who has gone fishing in Alaska for two weeks. Theresa begs and pleads, but because she has no *legal* relationship to Ernie, the hospital may be unable to perform surgery, or may have to wait to execute certain procedures. If our hypothetical clumsy carpenter, Ernie, had simply married Theresa, he would still have the use of his hypothetical right hand.

"But I'm not planning to saw off my hand," you complain, and you correctly point out that doctors in many states will perform emergency surgery without authorization. All right, assume that instead of sawing off his hand, Ernie saws off his stubborn unmarried head. Marriage obviously won't help *him* now, but what about Theresa's plight? After the coroners rush Ernie away in a couple of bags, Theresa is left in legal limbo. She cannot collect any insurance or other survivor's benefits from Ernie's work, or from Social Security. If Theresa's name is not on the deed to their house, she may have to move out and surrender all of Ernie's belongings to the legal next of kin (as soon as he gets back from Alaska). "Just living together" can become a legal quagmire compared to marriage.

Besides the legal advantages of being able to authorize surgery, collect survivor's benefits, and have quick answers to next-of-kin questions, married couples enjoy a long tradition of legal precedents regarding other situations. Whether buying a house, adopting a child, or applying for insurance, the married couple usually has a simpler time of things than do mere POSSLQs. The reason? While states merely tolerate "living together," they often go out of their way to protect marriage.

Tying the knot may also get you lower medical and auto

insurance premiums. Insurance companies recognize that, statistically, married people live longer, stay in better health, and have fewer car accidents. The insurers don't care why—all they know is that as a group, married people are a better risk. It pays to notify insurers of your change in marital status. They'll probably *lower* your rates.

LEGAL RESPONSIBILITIES

Death

Passing on, meeting your maker—whatever you choose to call it, death is not the most popular subject for consideration when preparing for a joyous event like a wedding. However (and hopefully this book is not the first place you discover it), you eventually are going to die. Since it's unlikely that you'll get advance notice about the particulars of when and how you're going to buy the farm, you want to make sure that your wife (children, parents, et cetera) will be protected whenever "it" happens. Making a will is the ultimate selfless act. Neglecting to make a will, or making a stupid (legally problematic) will, can be the ultimate foolish act.

When you die (forget that insurance salesman's favorite qualifier, "If, God forbid . . ." because you *are* going to die), all your *stuff* will still remain. Maybe you don't own too much now—but you're not planning on sawing off any limbs next week, either. By the time the inevitable finally occurs, you may have bought a house, won the lottery, or earned some financial credit in an employee retirement plan. If you've made no formal preparations before you die (if you die "intestate," as the lawyers say), that invisible partner in marriage, the state, marches in like a referee and starts dictating what becomes of your possessions.

If you have not made out a will, your things will be distributed according to *arbitrary rules* that are different depending on where you live. The state may also take a sizable cut for itself. Avoiding taking the time to write a will doesn't keep you from dying; rather, it means that through inaction you've agreed to let the state make all your decisions for you, whether or not that's in the best interests of your wife and other survivors. If you intend to leave everything to your wife, you'd better write a will, because the state may have other plans.

The do-it-yourself-will kits may be legal, may work fairly well, and may end up costing your survivors lots of money and heartache in legal complications and taxes paid unnecessarily. After you die, they might eulogize your shortsighted enthusiasm for doing it yourself by saying, "He saved five hundred bucks by writing his own will, and we have to pay an extra ten thousand in taxes!" Besides just splitting up your property among heirs (". . . and to my loving wife Elizabeth I leave the power tools . . ."), a good will should protect your heirs from having to pay unnecessary taxes.

The state has an ever-changing bag of tricks seemingly designed to separate your heirs from their property. In addition to inheritance taxes, which you've probably heard of, the state may make your widow pay an income tax on the increased value of your house. For example: You buy a house for $80,000 next year, and put it in your own name. Ten years from now you die (okay, let's be nice—*eighty* years from now—it doesn't really matter), without having written a proper will. She inherits the house, which in the year 2070 is worth $800,000. When she sells it, she may have to pay *income tax* on the increased price of the house—$720,000—even though it's still the same old house! Careful estate planning can prevent such expensive hassles.

The examples could go on forever. Every couple's situation is different, and most people's finances constantly change, as do state laws. The goal is to make sure that as much of your stuff as possible goes to the people you want to have it, not to the tax man. It's important to find out what the legal weather is in your state, and what kind of umbrella you require in order to stay out of the rain.

Fortunately, there are extremely clever folks who make it their business to know all these rules and will help a newly-wed couple optimize their situation. They're called lawyers. A good family lawyer can take into consideration all the details of your situation and direct you to the best course of action in terms of getting things to the people you want to receive them, and keeping it out of the hands of the state. Sometimes, the best solution isn't even a will but a legal construction called a Revocable Living Trust. By setting up a trust, you give all your assets to a legal structure called a "trust," which technically owns them. You're just the controller of the trust (which is as good as owning it), and when you die, the next trustee takes control. This may be a wise way to do things, particularly for couples who are financially privileged, wealthy, or just plain filthy rich. A lawyer can explain this option and its benefits and drawbacks.

If you have a will that was drawn up before you got married, it may now be null and void (the lawyers' way of saying "worthless"). Many states have a provision for "pretermitted heirs," which means that a will written without considering your spouse will be ignored. This places your survivors back at square one: The state comes in and divides up your goodies according to *its* rules, and uses your old will for scrap paper. Be sure to reexamine any existing will in light of your upcoming marriage.

Taxes

Almost as unpleasant as death in the mind of the groom is Ben Franklin's other great inevitable: taxes. Anyone who has ever filled out a W-4 knows that the IRS inquires as to your marital status. This is not required so that the IRS can send out anniversary cards to happy couples across the land. Rather, the amount of taxes withheld from your wages, and the rate of income tax you pay, changes according to whether you're married or single. Your tax status for the entire year is dictated by your status on December 31; so a marriage on New Year's Eve will affect the tax rate for the entire preceding year. For some couples the taxes paid according to the "married" rates are slightly higher (the so-called marriage penalty), so if your accountant determines that this is the case in your situation, it could save you some money to delay the wedding till after the first of the year.

Besides income taxes, as you progress in life, you may end up buying a house, owning a small business, or even becoming head of International Business Machines. As the stakes get higher, there are more opportunities to prevent chunks of your wealth from going to the tax man. A good certified public accountant or an estate planner can help keep newlyweds from feeling the pinch of unnecessary taxation.

What If We Get Married out of State or out of the Country?

As long as the marriage is legal and is *correctly recorded* where it occurs, every state in the union will recognize your union. The hitch? If you go to Paco's Wedding Chapel & Chicken Fights in Tijuana, or to a justice of the peace who has questionable credentials, the officiant may never bother to make an official record of your marriage. Since marriage is between two people and a state, if you have any doubt about the legitimacy of your ceremony, write to the appropriate recordkeeping office where you were married and request an official copy of the certificate. It is rare, but occasionally couples "married" forty years find out that technically they have been living out of wedlock because their marriage was not legally recorded.

What Is Common-Law Marriage?

Nine states plus the District of Columbia recognize common-law marriage, which is a legally sanctioned marriage that comes into being without a formal ceremony or license. There are many myths about common-law marriage, such as the belief that a man and woman must live together for seven years before such a union exists. The laws vary from state to state, but in some places, merely asking a woman, "Will you marry me?" and getting a yes is enough to be considered legally wed. Usually the couple must present themselves to the world as husband and wife and agree that they are married.

Once a common-law marriage exists in one state, every other state will recognize it. If you suspect that you or your fiancée may have entered into a common-law marriage agreement with someone else, research the particular details and consult a lawyer. If it turns out to be the awful truth, a divorce is required before another wedding (yours) can occur. One famous case involved an actor who lived with a woman in a common-law state for four months while shooting a film; that woman sued for alimony and claimed that his subsequent marriage to another woman was illegal. The tabloids call him "The Accidental Bigamist."

WHAT DO MY FIANCÉE AND I NEED TO DO BEFORE GETTING MARRIED?

Plenty of couples have gotten to the church only to find out that they haven't jumped through the right hoops in order to get married (legally). A ceremony by a minister is usually just icing on the cake and does not guarantee a legal marriage. Since laws vary from state to state, you need to check with the local courthouse to determine what needs to be done; otherwise, you may end up delaying the wedding unnecessarily. Usually, it's necessary to obtain a marriage license— essentially, permission from the state to get married, and the main way in which marriages are recorded. There is often a fee. Most states require that both partners be at least a certain age, usually eighteen. Some states will let younger people marry, provided they have the permission of their legal guardians. Many states require a blood test for syphilis, rubella, and in Illinois, AIDS, which can take two days to a week to obtain, so be sure to plan ahead.

If it's a second marriage for either partner, you'll need written proof of divorce before you are issued a marriage license. You'll also need positive identification. In some states there is a waiting period before obtaining a wedding license or between issuance of the license and the marriage. Other states issue wedding licenses for periods as short as thirty days—so it's crucial to plan a visit to the courthouse within that window of opportunity to ensure that you don't arrive at the chapel with an expired license.

Celebrate Getting the License

If you want to look really good in your fiancée's eyes, be prepared to pay the fee, make sure that you both have everything you need, and then plan a big date immediately afterward. Getting a wedding license is a milestone, and even if it's a dusty old courthouse covered with pigeon droppings, in a bad part of town, the trip to get the wedding license can be fun for both of you.

What About Children?

If you or your fiancée has children, no legal relationship automatically exists between the stepparent and stepchildren, unless the stepparent adopts them. States recognize the rights of the natural parents first and foremost, except in extreme cases, such as if the other parent is in jail or an insane asylum.

PRENUPTIAL AGREEMENTS

On TV and in the movies, prenuptial agreements are evil documents written up between a rich spouse and a poor spouse, saying in effect that if they should divorce, the rich spouse will keep all of his or her money and the poor spouse will be left with nothing. In actual practice, prenuptial agreements cover a wide variety of situations and are rarely so melodramatic.

A prenuptial agreement often has more to do with protecting both partners' possessions than anything else. The day you get married, some things that were once yours, or hers,

Sure, the courthouse is decrepit, the clerks officious, and the paperwork intimidating. But getting your wedding license is still cause to celebrate.

alone may become yours and your wife's. The laws regarding what is called community property, marital property, or equitable property are as arbitrary as inheritance laws and could create problems in your marriage or when the marriage ends, either by death or by divorce. Familiarize yourself with those laws in your state, and work to create the best situation possible for you and your wife.

People who sign prenuptial agreements are not planning to get divorced; more often, they are interested in protecting children, wealth, or businesses from the arbitrary laws of the state. For example: Jane is a doctor, part of a medical partnership. Joe is an attorney, a partner in his firm. In some states, by getting married Jane and Joe would each automatically become co-owners of each other's stake in their respective companies. To keep things from getting wildly complicated, they sign a prenuptial agreement that says, in twenty-six complicated pages of small print, what is hers remains hers and what is his remains his once they're married.

Another example: Frieda has two children and created a savings fund for them to go to college. She's marrying Don, a nice guy who has a lot of debts relating to a failed business. Depending on the laws of the state, Don's creditors may attempt to take Frieda's savings to pay Don's bills. A prenuptial agreement can keep their assets (and liabilities) separate and protect her children's future.

Some types of prenuptial agreements are written to make sure that both spouses' properties are mixed together, rather than keeping them separate. This is the exact opposite of the type of agreement portrayed in movies, and can serve to protect children, to make the legal details of a spouse's death easier, or even to make it easier to get a home loan.

The "rich spouse, poor spouse" type of prenuptial agreement makes better Hollywood fiction than it does law. Even if such a contract is drafted, a judge may throw it out if the "poor spouse" didn't understand its terms or didn't have adequate legal counsel when signing it. If you feel a need for such an agreement, be certain that both you and your fiancée have separate attorneys advising you, or the agreement may be ruled worthless.

The necessity for a prenuptial agreement is similar to the necessity for a will: If you have no property or children, or are totally satisfied with your state's laws concerning property and marriage, you probably don't need one. But if you or your fiancée owns a lot of property, or has debts or any other complicating situations, make sure that your "stuff" will be protected.

If the need does arise for a prenuptial agreement, present it to your fiancée diplomatically. Don't grab some papers and say, "Sign this." Rather, explain yourself: "I love you very much, _____(her name here). But I want to make sure my children/parents/business partners are protected, so I want to talk to a lawyer to make sure we haven't neglected something that could become a problem later for little Debbie/Gramps/ the company."

HOW TO FIND A GOOD FAMILY LAWYER

It's as important to spend time picking a lawyer as it is shopping for a new car. When someone can help (or hurt) you and your family as much as a lawyer has the potential to, you should have some reassurance that they really know what they're doing. The age-old question, "How can I tell a good one from a bad one?" is as difficult to answer when hiring a lawyer as when buying a canned ham. J. C. Hearsch, an attorney specializing in family law, offers some helpful advice on choosing a family lawyer.

1. Consider a potential attorney's reputation in the community. The best recommendation you can have for an attorney is the glowing testimonial of a satisfied client. Ask around: Perhaps your parents, your boss, or a friend has had a good experience working with an attorney and can make a recommendation. When asking around, make sure

that your friend got the same sort of legal advice you're looking for—an excellent patent attorney may be a terrible family lawyer.

2. If you can get no such recommendation, call the local Bar Association, which likely will have a Family Law Section. If it has no such group, you can obtain a list of members of the American Bar Association Family Law Section. Members either practice family law exclusively or devote a good portion of their time to it and will know the legal situation in your state.

3. Once you've narrowed your search to family lawyers gleaned from the Bar Association or a friend, you can find out how good a particular lawyer is by looking in the Martindale-Hubble Directory, which rates lawyers in much the same way as Consumer Reports rates cars (except there are no crash tests for lawyers, yet). Where can you find the Martindale-Hubble Directory? Try the library of a university law school, or call your public library, which, if they don't have a copy, will be able to tell you where to find one.

4. The final test in choosing a lawyer is personal preference. Ask how much experience the attorney has had in family law. Ask how much it will cost to prepare the documents you want. And whenever you run across something you don't understand, ask for it to be explained in simple terms. A good lawyer should make things clear and understandable for you rather than obfuscating matters in legal jargon. Your attorney should act as an interpreter between you and the law, not as some sort of voodoo priest throwing out multisyllabic words and chanting "trust me, trust me."

Source for further information: the American Bar Association publishes a pamphlet entitled "Love, Marriage and The Law," which can be obtained for $3.50 (postpaid) from the American Bar Association, Order Fulfillment, 1155 East 60th Street, Chicago, IL 60637.

9

MOVING IN

With house prices skyrocketing, some newlyweds opt for extremely small starter homes. Roof optional.

Unless you and your fiancée already live together, moving in together may be the first genuine hard work of your marriage. No other prenuptial activity presents quite the same opportunities for wheeling and dealing, injured backs, and revelation of the surprising disagreements you can have with your bride. Choosing the kind of home you'd like to live in is an extremely personal matter, and in the quest for the first marital homestead (or apartmentstead) your values and those of your fiancée may meet in a head-to-head battle of primeval forces.

Ricardo, a Miami investment analyst, hadn't given much thought to what kind of place to get, but when he started looking for an apartment with Sibyl, his fiancée, who worked as a lifeguard, he discovered that he held definite opinions on what made a good apartment, and Sibyl thought they were all wrong. Ricardo had picked out a place with a weight room near his downtown office, but Sibyl hated it because she wanted to live by the beach in a place that would let her keep her three cats. Even though he'd put down a deposit on the place, he had to sacrifice it, because he had jumped the gun and hadn't considered Sibyl's opinion on the apartment.

To find out what's important to you, and to your fiancée, rate the following home characteristics in order of their importance, and have your fiancée do the same. You may be startled at the differences, and it should lead to an interesting discussion on the merits of different places to live. Number the items on each list, with 1 being the most important to you, 2 second most important, and so on. Unless you're rich you will have to sacrifice something, and you and your fiancée will probably order the lists differently.

Rooms (rank In Importance, 1 to 5):
____ Big closets
____ Big kitchen
____ Big dining area
____ Big bedroom
____ Big bathroom
____ (fill in) _____

Location (rank In Importance, 1 to 5):
____ Near to my work
____ Near to my parents/friends
____ Near parks and recreation
____ Near groceries and shopping
____ Near movies and nightlife
____ (fill in) _____

Extras (rank In Importance, 1 to 5):
____ A pool
____ Lots of sunlight and windows
____ A balcony
____ A good view
____ Secured parking
____ Conveniences like dishwashers and microwaves
____ Nice carpets, drapes, and decor
____ Extra room for workshop or study room
____ (fill in) _____

Quality of Life (rank in importance, 1 to 5):

____ In a safe part of town

____ Quiet, away from busy streets and noisy neighbors

____ Private enough to blast the stereo

____ Allows pets

____ (fill in) _____

Hobbies and Spare Time Use (write in):

In my private time, I hope to _____

_____

There are no right or wrong answers; the test is simply to help you assess what you and your fiancée each feel is important. You both may have to make some compromises; consider it good training for marriage.

GETTING A NEW PLACE TOGETHER

When to Move in

The exact timing of the move-in is an art, not a science. In the busy period around a wedding, moving is the last thing you have time for, and yet there are arguments to be made in favor of moving as close to the time of the wedding as possible. It gives you a sense of starting a new life together, and in spite of the time constraint, the effort may be worth it. Alternatively, moving long in advance can save on rent and get a burden out of the way sooner. Moving some time after the wedding lets you concentrate on the ceremony and lets you shop for an apartment calmly after the dust has settled.

MOVING IN WAY BEFORE THE WEDDING

Advantages:

It gets a big chunk of work out of the way far in advance of the busy wedding time.

You'll be together while planning the wedding and able easily to confer on a variety of tasks.

You won't be paying double rent.

Disadvantages:

Both you and your fiancée won't be able to enjoy the "final days of singlehood" apart from each other.

If buying a house, the task is more complicated for two single persons than for a married couple (see Chapter 8, "The Law").

Many religions, not to mention parents and conservative relatives, frown on cohabiting before the wedding. You also might end up fighting about the color of the toilet paper on the day of the wedding, which could put a damper on the proceedings.

MOVING IN TOGETHER
NEAR THE TIME OF THE WEDDING

Advantages:

A sense of starting a new life together comes with moving in near the time of the wedding. You may also have lots of nifty new wedding presents to furnish your home. Plus, the glitz of the wedding can provide a nice antidote to the drudgery of moving.

Disadvantages:

Of course, time is at a premium during the final countdown. In addition to wedding showers, out-of-town guests, and the whole ball of wax, you have the added burden of hauling all your stuff from point A to point B.

MOVING IN AFTER THE WEDDING

Advantages:

You have all the wedding
festivities out of the way before
you move, and you already
have the majority of your
wedding gifts.

Disadvantages:

You won't have a new home to
go to after the honeymoon; in
fact, you'll have an incredible
amount of work to do when
you get back.

SHE'S MOVING INTO MY PLACE

If you're not choosing a new home together, there are still
emotional land mines waiting to blow up in your face. If she's
moving into your apartment, it's extremely important to back
off from the "my home, my castle" caveman attitude toward
your abode and let her make her mark. Try to clear out at
least half the closets, and seek out her opinion on decor.
Making her feel welcome is not nearly enough. She has to feel
it's *her* place too, and that she's got more authority over the
surroundings than would a mere guest. It may even mean
letting her take your treasured space-shuttle pictures (not to
mention Miss September) off the walls.

Whether she moves into your place, you into hers, or you
already live together, it's worth going the extra mile to make
your new life together as a married couple seem different,
better, and special. When both partners move, they get the
opportunity to start anew by default; in other situations, it
takes ingenuity to make the marital home seem different.
Leon, a Detroit contractor, and his fiancée, Nella, a hair-
dresser, had lived together for two years before tying the knot.
Nella decided to spend the week before the wedding at her
sister's house, to have a last week of "just us girls" before the
big change. Leon, a first-rate groom if ever there was one,
took the initiative and repainted the rooms in their house,
installed a chandelier, and got a new sign for the door that
said MR. & MRS. He kept Nella away by pretending to have a
wild week-long fling with the boys, so she didn't even see his

handiwork till after the honeymoon. When she entered their "new and improved" house, she made all his labor worthwhile by shrieking with delight nonstop while dancing from room to room, then giving Leon a huge hug as tears of joy ran down her face. It wasn't the painting that pleased her so; it was the intention behind it. Nella knew that Leon cared, and that he was happily making the change from "just living together" to marriage.

It's not necessary to go to incredible extremes, nor does your effort have to be a surprise. What's important is that you make a change in the way you think about your surroundings. It's no longer just a place to live. It's a home.

WHAT'S IT GOING TO COST?

You've looked at apartments high and low. The decision is now between two apartments, similar in many respects, that both you and your fiancée like. One costs fifty dollars less per month, is in a slightly worse neighborhood, and is farther from both of your jobs, but the other, more-expensive apartment includes utilities as part of the rent. Which is a better deal?

The naïve apartment shopper believes that the sole bottom line is the amount of rent paid. Low rent can be a false economy. When comparing the costs of apartments, several factors besides rent should be taken into account. These include the costs of utilities, of renters' insurance, of auto insurance, and of commuting to work.

When a landlord does not pay utilities, you must add the price of electricity, gas, water, and sewer to the cost of rent when comparing it with a "utilities included" apartment. If the building owner is not forthcoming with this information, check with a resident in a similar unit, or if possible with the previous tenant of the apartment you wish to rent. Sometimes the utilities companies themselves will help you "guesstimate" the average monthly bill. For heating costs, take the average of winter and summer figures to derive a realistic average toll.

In most states, renters' insurance (which insures your personal property if you should be robbed or if the place burns down, as well as providing some liability coverage) and auto insurance quotes are tied to ZIP codes. The underwriters' argument is that people in certain parts of town are robbed more often and crash more cars than in other neighborhoods, and thus residents of those "bad" areas pay more for their insurance. If you're looking in several neighborhoods, check with an insurance agent to find out the rate for auto and home liability in each. Due to the vagaries of actuarial tables, sometimes a difference in location of one block can save more than $100 per month in insurance costs.

Finally, consider the driving distance to both of your jobs. Operating a car costs about 20 cents a mile. Someone will argue, "But I get thirty miles a gallon and gas is a dollar a gallon so I don't have to pay that much," but the truth is that a car does not last forever, and there are many other expenses besides gasoline. Figuring in the costs of oil changes, the inevitable breakdowns, tires, and eventually having to buy another car, 20 cents a mile is probably low. Based on 20 cents per mile, times five hundred trips per year, divided by twelve months, commuting costs about $12.50 per month, per mile driven one way to work. If your work is ten miles away, commuting costs about $125 per month. If your wife's job is twenty miles away, it costs another $250 per month for her. In its fundamentals, a mile closer to work is worth about $12.50 per month in rent and other expenses. For bus and train users, add in the monthly cost of tickets instead of the automobile costs.

Most landlords and home economists agree that the amount of money spent for rent should not exceed one-quarter to one-third of a couple's combined take-home pay. "Take-home" pay is the amount you get to deposit into the bank after all the taxes and deductions have been extracted by your employer. If you and your wife each bring home $300 a week, your combined monthly take-home pay would be $2,400, and the upper limit of rent (or mortgage payments) should be $600 to $800.

PRIVATE TIME/PRIVATE SPACE

Getting married is the "great union" of two individuals. How-ever, when choosing a place to live, do not overlook the necessity for a little separation amid all that togetherness. No matter how humble your first digs together are, you and your fiancée should consider the activities you enjoy during your personal time.

Marv and Beverly worked together in a Salt Lake City pharmaceutical laboratory, had a fine romance, and quickly got married. Marv had a passion for building model planes; Bev taught a Bible class, in her home, to emotionally disturbed children. The one-room flat they rented seemed like a warm first home, and Marv imagined he'd help out with the kids. He quickly discovered that he didn't have the patience to work with the children, nor did he get the same satisfaction from it as Bev did. In addition, when she was teaching (which began to seem like *all the time!*) he had to put the model pieces away or risk their destruction. When he'd take them back out later, there'd always seem to be a missing piece anyway. If he left them out, she complained that he was in the way of her classes. After their first lease was up, they moved to a place with two rooms, which gave them the opportunity to pursue their free-time activities independently. All it took to keep Marv happy was a three-square-foot table all his own.

It's the little things that drive a person crazy. Be sure to consider how you each spend your independent time. Too much togetherness can lead to ugly, unnecessary fights. If you jog, be sure you have a place to hang out your socks; if you read late at night, be sure there's somewhere to finish a novel without keeping your new bride awake. Before you start apartment hunting, think about how you each spend your evenings and weekends and what kind of extra room that would require.

Be sure to communicate to your fiancée any designs you have on a potential home. Harley and Dorothy both were elated with the two-bedroom apartment they'd found. The plan was that one bedroom would be used for sleeping and the other one would be a workroom. Dorothy planned to set up *her* worktable in the spare room, where she laid out photos and drew sketches. Harley imagined having a little "men's club" room, where he could put *his* computer and desk and a little couch. Neither told the other of these plans. They moved from two separate apartments, and on moving day, box after box and most of the furniture ended up cluttering the ten-by-eight-foot space. Only after there were two desks, a couch, a bed, file cabinets, and several dressers in the "spare room" did they realize that each had visualized the space differently, and that all that stuff would never fit in there. The rest of the apartment was nearly empty. Harley and Dorothy are still trying to find an adequate compromise, and some of the sheen is off of their "perfect" apartment.

A good way to make sure that both you and your fiancée understand plans for a home (before moving) is to sketch out a floor plan. On graph paper, draw a scale map of the apartment. Although any scale will work, five feet to the inch gives enough detail to enable you to make good decisions. For instance, if a wall in the apartment is ten feet long, make it two inches long on the graph paper. Then, using the same scale, make cut-out paper representations of all the furniture you plan to put in the apartment. You can try out alternate furniture configurations on paper, which is much easier than hauling real furniture around. It also can be a guide to what to throw away or store—a scale map may reveal that there is just no room at all for the air-hockey table *and* the pinball machine in a one-bedroom apartment.

MOVING

Figure out how long you think it will take to pack, then double the estimate. It always takes longer. Movers usually will sell you cartons, but for most purposes free boxes from liquor stores work better. A carton that holds a case of beer bottles is just about the right size to fill with books or cooking utensils.

If you're not using a mover, be sure to rent a hand truck and packing blankets. The extra ten bucks is a pittance compared to expensive back surgery. Put the largest objects into the truck first; cartons and boxes can fit on top of them. Have one "vital" box that contains the things you'll need on the way and immediately upon arrival, including identification papers, bank information, toothbrushes and toilet kits, and a change of clothes for each of you.

SPECIAL ADVICE IF YOU'RE MOVING OUT OF TOWN

There are special demands to be met if you plan to move a long distance. Often, it's impossible for both people to hunt for an apartment together, so it's more important than ever to discuss what you'd each like in the home; and there must be a way to communicate what the potential choices are like. Try taking photos (see "Photographing Potential Homes the Professional Way," p. 116) of potential choices so that the person who can't go along will get a clear picture of what the place is like. No matter how thoroughly a site is described in words, a photo shows details that the person visiting the site might not have considered important.

When moving out of town, it's extremely important to estimate how many things you'll be moving. It's not as if you can take a second trip. Use the paper cut-outs of furniture you've made to estimate the size of truck required, then add in some extra room for things forgotten.

Before leaving, make sure that there are hotels along the way (if the trip is more than one day long) and that they are in reasonably safe neighborhoods. The American Automobile Association can assist with routing and hotel reservations. Remember: You won't always find a hotel at the last minute. It always seems there's an Elk's convention in the town you hope to stay in overnight.

If you have two cars and a rental moving truck, you'll need either three drivers, a way to tow one of the cars, or someone to ship the extra car. The *Yellow Pages* lists auto-shipping companies that will take a car to any point for a reasonable fee, usually using trucks returning empty after delivering new cars.

SMARTNESS BOX
How Much Does That Apartment *Really* Cost?

Monthly rent $_____
Average of winter and summer *utilities* $_____
For that neighborhood, cost of *car insurance* $_____
For that neighborhood, cost of *home insurance* $_____
Number of miles to your work one way × $12.50 $_____
Number of miles to fiancée's work one way × $12.50 $_____

Total: How much does that apartment really cost? $_____

BONUS SMARTNESS BOX
Safe Lifting of Heavy Objects

You get only one spine. If you're moving lots of heavy furniture in hopes of impressing your new wife, make sure not to throw out your back. Groaning in bed with a slipped disk can be hazardous to your sex life. Chiropractors recommend you lift in the following way: Get as close as possible to the heavy object (say a box of records or books), and squat down, separating your knees. Your feet should be far enough apart that they're approximately underneath your shoulders. The box should be between your knees. Lift using the muscles in your legs—which can handle the weight—and not with the back, which can't. Hold heavy objects close to the body, and be sure the path to where you'll put it down is clear. If you can't see over an object, have someone lead you.

For furniture and other large objects, try to use smarts, not brute force, to get them around. Placing a mover's furniture pad under a desk will allow you to slide it across a hardwood floor. A hand truck will let you take advantage of the cave-man's big contribution to society, the wheel. If you have trouble lifting something, get assistance. Especially on busy days, a great temptation is to just force it up, but back injuries and hernias are often waiting for those who rush.

A good way to get information about a new town is through its Chamber of Commerce or Welcome Wagon association. They will usually provide maps, coupons to local businesses, and vital information such as the phone numbers for utility companies, hospitals, and police and fire departments.

This may seem as cryptic as working out the new tax forms, but it will give you an accurate estimate of the cost of a particular apartment. To figure the commuting cost, take the number of miles driven one way to work, and multiply that figure by $12.50. For example, if you drive seven miles to work, it will cost you approximately $87.50 per month to drive to and from work. If you walk to work, you can enter a zero. If you commute by bus or train, use the monthly cost of the tickets.

APARTMENT HUNTING TIPS

1. Check the water pressure in any apartment or house you're serious about. Several years of dribbling low-pressure showers can make an otherwise good place extremely annoying—and no matter how nice a place looks, unless you turn the faucet you'll have no inkling that the pressure might be bad till that first lousy shower after you move in.

2. Find out how soon the rent can be raised and how much of an increase is likely. In some cities without rent control, attractive rents are offered at first, but drastic rent increases are charged as soon as the first rental agreement expires. A long lease has the advantage of locking in your rate for the length of the agreement.

3. Read the lease carefully. Before signing, you can and should cross out anything you don't like. For example, many standard rental forms forbid the tenant from nailing anything to the wall, or from ever having an overnight guest not named on the lease. The landlord might not kick you out for breaking such a clause but can use it against you if he or she has a grudge. In cities with rent control, research the laws to find out how you as a tenant may be protected; checking with the local Tenants' Association is a good way to start your research.

Check the water pressure of any apartment before paying a deposit.

4. When you find a place you might take, don't be pressured into signing right away. Come back at odd times of day to check the neighborhood and the noise levels. What looks like a nice apartment at 10:00 A.M. might be a noisy, smelly quagmire at 7:00 P.M.

5. Find out where you'll park. For places that offer no parking, find out where you'll probably be able to park, and imagine carrying every bag of groceries you buy that distance.

6. Find the nearest grocery, drugstore, and gas station. An otherwise excellent apartment may be miles from any services.

7. Find out the total move-in cost. Tenants often have to pay first and last months' rent plus a security deposit, plus other deposits. A security deposit is usually refundable when

you move; a cleaning deposit is usually kept by the landlord. Ask what will be refunded.

8. Ask who does repairs. If a pipe bursts or some other misfortune occurs in the apartment, you should be assured of quick and reliable service to repair it. An on-site manager is a good sign that problems will be resolved quickly.

9. Finally, visualize how you'll live in the apartment, the way you lead your life. Do you watch a lot of TV? Mentally picture where the television will go and where the couch will go. Does your fiancée have a home computer? Where will its desk go, and where can you plug it in? Do out-of-town guests stay over often? Where will they sleep? Whatever you and your fiancée like to do, stand in a prospective apartment and imagine how you'll accomplish it in the given space. This will point out subtle problems before you sign the lease. For example, a Seattle couple heavily into sports was almost ready to sign a lease when they realized that there was not nearly enough space to store their gear, and (gasp!) that there was no cable TV, thus no twenty-four-hour sports channel. They chose another apartment.

PHOTOGRAPHING POTENTIAL HOMES
THE PROFESSIONAL WAY

If you're moving out of town, or schedules prevent you and your fiancée from looking for a place together, it's possible to use a video camera to document the insides of apartments or houses so that you can look at them together on a later date. Or, using an ordinary camera, photograph potential pads the professional-movie-location-manager way. Simply take a picture, turn so you get the next piece of room (without moving from your spot) and snap another picture, and continue till you have captured the whole area. Later, paste the photos together in a folder side by side, and attach other relevant information, such as cost, landlord, et cetera.

With these photo panoramas, you can compare several homes at a glance.

For the place you eventually choose, save the photos or

videotape you made. In addition to being a fun document of your love nest, they serve as excellent evidence of the original condition of the apartment or house if you ever have trouble recovering a security deposit from a landlord (e.g., the peanut butter on the walls was there when you moved in).

ONCE YOU'VE FOUND A PLACE: A MOVING CHECKLIST

____ Change of address. If your wife (or you) will be changing names, be sure to note that. Change-of-address cards can be obtained from the post office and should be sent to:

Current job
Previous jobs (if you've recently changed jobs, the former employer still needs the new address to mail tax forms at the end of the year)
Magazine subscriptions
Bank: checking, savings
Bank credit cards
Store credit cards
Place of worship
College or university alumni association
Family
Friends
Doctor
Draft registration board (required by law for men ages 18 to 25)
Department of Motor Vehicles
Insurance companies
State tax boards; IRS (with Social Security number)

____ Disconnect gas, electric, cable TV, and water at previous places and pay final bill
____ Arrange for utilities to be started at new home
____ Make keys for you and fiancée/wife, as well as extra set
____ Return library books
____ Pick up laundry

10

GETTING
DRESSED

COURTESY OF AFTER SIX FORMALS®

One of the major differences between a wedding and a fashion show is that at the fashion show the models don't have to pay for the clothes they wear. Many types of weddings aren't influenced by current trends at all, and the question, "What is Fashion?" mercifully doesn't enter the picture. Military men can wear their dress uniforms; some religions have ceremonial garb that is worn at a wedding; and certain ethnic groups have traditional clothing that is especially for nuptials. However, if you're like the majority of grooms in the United States, you need to buy a nice suit or rent or buy some formal wear. To do so, it helps to have some insight into the forces that influence a "proper" choice.

"Proper" means "fashionable," which means "whatever the fashion people decide." "The fashion people" are a secretive group of designers, magazine editors, and marketing mavens who annually arrive at a consensus of sorts on what is in fashion and what is out of fashion, as arbitrarily and mysteriously as the oracles at Delphi. They are answerable to no one, they are free to flop back and forth annually between designs, and yet their aesthetic whims may as well be law.

Some common questions about fashion can be answered easily: Why was last year's fabric smooth, and this year's fabric seersucker (or the other way around)? *Because it is.* Why was last year's formal wear two-tone, and this year a single color is in (or vice versa)? *Because it is.* Why is wearing a vest coming back in (or going back out)? *Because it is.*

At a military wedding, the dress uniform is worn.
UCLA

Attempting to find any logic or pattern in the dictates of fashion will prove fruitless, and yet the groom should pay close attention to what is in fashion and what is out. As Thomas Jefferson (a guy who got married)* said, "In matters of principle, stand like a rock; in matters of taste, swim with the current."

How does the groom find out which way the current is flowing? Do not ask your father, unless you want to wear something six years out of date. Do not go on your own instincts, unless you want to wear something that looks like it came off of "The Love Boat" (the source of many half-baked notions about romance and formal wear). An excellent source of insider information about current fashion is that stack of magazines your fiancée has accumulated, all of which have the word *Bride* in the title.

---

*Okay, he wrote the Declaration of Independence, too, and was president. But we're talking fashion, not history, here.

The copy that goes with the photos may read something like this: *"This year, white—beautiful, solid, dependable, ineffable white—is back in style. Like the birds returning to Capistrano, the dependable, clean-cut look of white is back once again, and is a welcome addition to the menswear scene."* Reducing it to its simplest form, the groom can deduce, "White = Fashion = A Good Thing."

Your bride may be more attuned to what's in and what's out, and it can be as fun to consult with her about formal wear as it was to consult with her about housewares. Flipping through the pages of bridal magazines and tuxedo-company brochures, one can pretty accurately take the national formal-wear pulse and pick this year's style.

If opening the bridal magazines is too difficult, the "tuxedo professionals" down at the local shop can generally fill you in on what's in and what's out. As with so many other wedding-

In matters of principle, stand like a rock; in matters of taste, swim with the current."

—Thomas Jefferson (not pictured)

related tasks, it's crucial to get to the formal-wear shop as far in advance as possible. There, they will measure your inseam and outseam, take a few other vital statistics, and reduce your physical dimensions down to a few numbers on an index card.

It may be tempting to take your own measurements or read them off of the leather tag sewn to a pair of old jeans. However, this is an extremely bad idea, and you may end up looking like Pee-Wee Herman, or David Byrne. Formal-wear measurements differ from those for jeans, since there's no shrinkage, and since they take an outseam as well as an inseam. The word on measuring yourself: "Kids, don't try this at home! We're trained professionals!"

The official party line on formal wear dictates what clothing can be worn at which time of day and is extremely complicated. For example, there are different rules for semiformal evening weddings held in summer and winter. (Of course you knew that. Who would ever dare to wear the same thing to a semiformal evening gathering in the summer as he'd wear to a winter semiformal evening affair? Hardly anyone.) Discovering the most "proper" choice is no more difficult than finding an obscure part for an Edsel in an auto-parts catalog. Use the dress chart to find out the rules, but once you've determined them, feel free to break every single one. Whatever you and your bride agree you should wear is the most important criterion. It's unlikely that anyone will jump up at the church and scream "foul" if you wear a tailcoat before 6:00 P.M. The formal-wear chart on pages 128–29 explains the rules.

When you make arrangements with the formal-wear shop, get their assurances that you can come in for a final fitting at least a couple of days before the wedding. Even after they've taken your measurements, formal-wear pros can only come close with a particular suit and will still need to adjust the hems. On the day of the wedding, you'll be too busy to care, and may end up having to hold your clothes together with Scotch tape and safety pins unless you can get a tailor to alter it. A reputable formal-wear shop will have a tailor on staff to do the job for you.

A note on Team Groom: Ideally, all the groomsmen should get their clothing at the same shop. Single-source buying can ensure that the colors will be coordinated and the suits will match. What one dealer calls "beige" may wind up as dark brown at another, and details such as the color of ties can be easily confused. It would look pretty silly for three groomsmen to have black trousers and the fourth to be in white.

Unless you explicitly offer to pay for all rented clothing, each member of your party is responsible for his own tab. You don't have to confront the groomsmen with this information; let the formal-wear dealer know that he should bill each man separately and he'll take care of it.

What are the stakes of executing this fashion mission? Picking his clothes is often the most highly visible role a groom has in the wedding. The first time many members of her family may lay eyes on him is at the altar, and they will judge him on his looks. If the groom looks as if he just got up, the relatives might think, *"What a twit!"* but if he truly looks sharp, they may err in the opposite direction and believe, *"Our girl married good. He'll probably win a Nobel Prize!"* All this, before he even utters a word.

PICKING A GOOD TUX DEALER

Is there such a thing as a "good" or a "bad" formal-wear dealer? Little clues may help you know when you've entered a decent tux shop or Formal Wear Hell. You drive to the first place you happen to hear of. It's incredibly dusty and dim, and the place smells like a locker that hasn't been opened in a while. Then, the leathery old proprietor—himself in an ill-fitting suit—proceeds to *tell* you what you should wear, holding a cigarette that's got about three inches of ash hanging off of it and looks ready to drop and ignite the place. "Everybody's wearing plaid this year. I should know. That's what you'll want. If you don't get plaid, you won't be happy, lemme tell you."

You actually were hoping for black tails, but as soon as you dare suggest this he throws his hands up in the air and scowls, "Black tails, black schmails. You want plaid, son, trust me. Everybody's wearing it." Who are these self-appointed arbiters of taste, and how do you avoid them? It's impossible to know ahead of time, so when caught in a bad tux shop, just say, "Thank you very much," and leave quickly. Even when a groom has a solid idea of what he wants to wear, a bad tuxedo pusher can wear him down quickly and create an undesirable compromise. Learn to recognize manipulation and stay away from manipulators.

What distinguishes a formal-wear professional from guys who happen to rent suits? Three things: service, service, and service. The price of renting formal wear may seem high in relation to the cost of purchasing (often 25 to 30 percent of the purchase price), so it's important for the groom to realize that his money should be paying for a lot more than just clothing. Following is a list of services that any reputable shop should deliver.

1. Listening to the groom. The formal-wear professional will listen to your needs and desires and provide you with clothing you desire. When you ask for recommendations, he should give the benefit of his experience and expertise, and then go with your wishes, whatever they are. A bad dealer will be dictatorial, telling you to wear what *he* thinks is right (which is often exactly what he has in stock). A good dealer should provide you with the accessories you need, not try to sell you goofy little knickknacks you don't want, or items you want to supply yourself, such as shoes. A dealer who tries to push you into something you don't want is a dealer to whom you don't want to give your business.

2. The science of tailoring. A former-wear professional should take all of your measurements (inseam, outseam, shirt size, et cetera) and keep track of all the sizes for your groomsmen, whether they come to his shop to be measured or are measured out of town by another tailor. If a man in your party has not sent in his measurements, the formal-wear professional should notify you in time to get them.

3. Test fitting and alterations. This may be the ultimate test of a good formal-wear supplier. He should agree to a test fitting, far enough in advance to make alterations if necessary or to order different clothing if alterations won't do. At least two days in advance of the wedding, the groom should be confident that he's going to look extremely sharp on the big day. At this time, all the accessories should be gathered together with the suit and kept in one place.

4. Excellence in clothing. The formal-wear you rent should be pressed, clean, and new-looking. Some "discount" or disreputable formal-wear dealers may supply you with less-than-perfect-looking duds. That's the last thing you need on your wedding day. If you have any doubts about a shop, ask to see something that they're sending out that day. It should look new. No excuses, no apologies, no justifications.

DRESS CHART

		Formal Evenings After 6 P.M. (Year 'round)	Semiformal Evening After 6 P.M. (Sept.–May)
COAT		Tailcoat (full dress)	Formal separate dinner jacket or tuxedo
COLOR		Black	Black or subdued colors to coordinate
TROUSERS		To match coat	To match or coordinate with coat
VEST		White piqué waistcoat	Matching or coordinated vest
SHIRT		White piqué bosom	Pleated or fancy bosom in white or colors
COLLAR		Wing (separate) or attached	Attached turndown or wing collar
TIE		White bow	Black or to match shirt, vest, or satin facings. Patterned or solid ascot
JEWELRY		White or pearl studs and links	Black, gold, or jeweled studs and links
SHOES		Patent pumps or oxfords	Patent or polished calf dress shoes
HOSE		Black silk, lisle, or nylon	Black silk, lisle, or nylon
OVERCOAT		Black dress coat	Black single- or double-breasted coat

COURTESY OF AFTER SIX FORMALS®

Semiformal Evening After 6 P.M. (May–Sept.)	Formal Daytime Before 6 P.M. (Year 'round)	Semiformal Daytime Before 6 P.M. (Year 'round)
Dinner jacket or tuxedo	Tuxedo, Ascot, or Classic Cutaway	Classic Stoller or the tuxedo of your choice
White, pastels, vibrant colors	The color of your choice	Gray (Stroller) or color of your choice (tux)
Black, or to match or coordinate with coat	Matching, coordinating, or Classic Stripe (with cutaway)	Matching, coordinating, or Classic Stripe
Plain or matching vest	Matching or coordinating vest	Matching or coordinating vest
Pleated or fancy bosom in white or colors	Your choice—plain or fancy—white or colors	Your choice—plain or fancy—white or colors
Attached turndown or wing collar	Wing or attached turndown collar	Wing or attached turndown collar
Black or to match shirt or vest. Patterned or solid ascot	Color-coordinated bow or striped or solid ascot	Color-coordinated bow or striped or solid ascot or four-in-hand
Black, gold, or jeweled studs and links	Pearl or jeweled stickpin with ascot	Black, gold, or jeweled studs and links
Patent or polished calf dress shoes	Polished calf dress shoes	Polished calf dress shoes
Black silk, lisle, or nylon	Black silk, lisle, or nylon	Black silk, lisle, or nylon
None	Black or oxford gray Chesterfield	Black or oxford gray Chesterfield

A Flow Chart

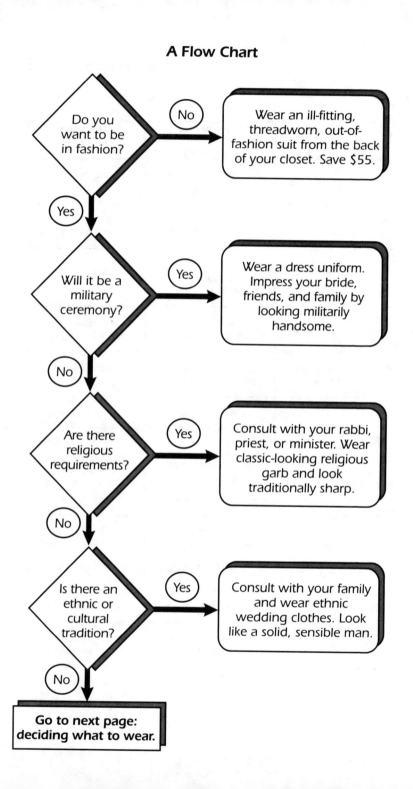

Do you want to be in fashion? — No → Wear an ill-fitting, threadworn, out-of-fashion suit from the back of your closet. Save $55.

Yes ↓

Will it be a military ceremony? — Yes → Wear a dress uniform. Impress your bride, friends, and family by looking militarily handsome.

No ↓

Are there religious requirements? — Yes → Consult with your rabbi, priest, or minister. Wear classic-looking religious garb and look traditionally sharp.

No ↓

Is there an ethnic or cultural tradition? — Yes → Consult with your family and wear ethnic wedding clothes. Look like a solid, sensible man.

No ↓

Go to next page: deciding what to wear.

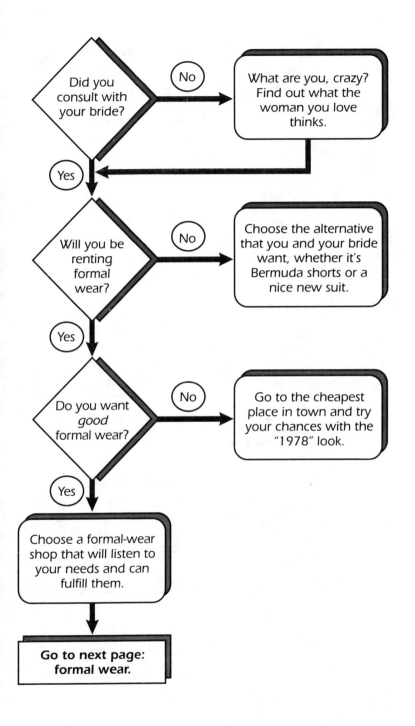

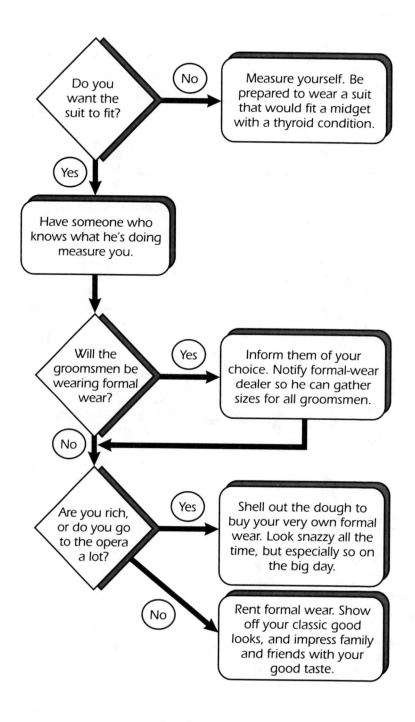

Tying a ''real'' bow tie is the simplest thing in the world. Just pull the ends apart, put a finger under one side, form a loop, pull through the loop, and, uh . . . Maybe it's not so simple.

Then again, really good clip-on bow ties are available in a wide variety of styles. They require no manual dexterity whatsoever.

11

THE
BACHELOR PARTY

This is what I remember about my bachelor party: Waking up under a spray of cold water from a sink at a laundromat, as the sun was rising. My buddies had apparently dragged me there, hoping to sober me up. The last thing I could tell you before that I was picking a fight with a Hell's Angel in Nudie Judy's Party Room, after the biker complained about my setting fire to a Garfield doll while doing The Twist standing on a table, dressed only in my boxer shorts.

—A groom we'll call "X," age 27

The best man arranged it all. In a private party house in the woods outside of town, he'd filled an entire bathtub with liquor, and we took turns dunking our heads in the tub and gulping it down. Later, we had some fun using a semiautomatic rifle to blow away a television set tuned to an Alan Alda movie. At exactly midnight, he wheeled in a gigantic cake, out of which jumped not one but six girls, some of whom did things I've only ever read about in books. I didn't know they still had those cakes.

—A groom we'll call "X minus 1," age 19

They blindfolded me and took me to a yacht. After sailing out past the coastal limit, they opened the main cabin, where every variety of illegal drug was

137

sitting on tables, with little signs saying "eat me," "drink me," and so on. I experimented with them all. We were worried when a coast-guard cutter flashed its searchlight on us, but then saw that its entire crew was beautiful young women, and they came on board and partied with us till dawn.

—A groom we'll call "X to the third power," age 33

These three tales of drunkenness, debauchery, and decadence illustrate the first and most important rule about your bachelor party: *Lie like a rug about what really happened.* No matter how dull it was, concoct the wildest possible misadventures to tell people. Every man present at the party must swear on a stack of Bibles never to tell what *actually* happened. Any inconsistencies in the stories originating from your bash can always be attributed to the supposed effects of drugs and/or alcohol.

Here's the straight dope on what *really* transpired at the bachelor parties described above: The groom who supposedly picked a fight with a Hell's Angel actually spent his bachelor party playing poker at the best man's apartment, where they consumed prodigious quantities of pizza and beer. The guy who claimed "six girls jumping out of a cake" really went with his best friends to see "Battle of the Monster Trucks" at the Coliseum, and afterward went to a coffeeshop and talked about their high-school days. The "coast-guard orgy" was in fact a beach barbecue, followed by a rousing game of all-night miniature golf.

To assist you in the creation of your own tale of excess and immorality, on pages 142–43 is the "Insanely Great Bachelor Party Machine," which will help you to include in your story the all-important elements of a dangerous-sounding bachelor party: drunkenness, unlawfulness, scantily clad bimbos, macho excess, random stupidity, and, finally, unconsciousness.

The creation of a wild bachelor-party story is a closely guarded male tradition, and the entire gender is dependent on each new groom to carry his own weight by maintaining the myth. Even if the truth about your party would make a

Is this what really happened at the bachelor party? Or is it just a good story?

AMERICAN STOCK PHOTOGRAPHY

decent story without embellishment, it is incumbent upon you and your groomsmen to make it sound as if you went to the edge of hell, picked a fight with Satan, won it, and came back smiling.

THE REAL BACHELOR PARTY

In the movies, the bachelor party is thrown by the best man on the night before the wedding. It's always shown as a gathering of the groomsmen (dressed in their tuxedos, of course) at some banquet room with ice sculpture where everyone knocks back highballs and eventually a babe better endowed than a blue-ribbon watermelon patch jumps out of a cake. Beyond the self-evident truth that ice sculpture is the nerdiest art form this side of mime, the popular conception of a bachelor party is wrong in almost all of its particulars:

Time. The bachelor party should be held sometime in the week or so before the wedding, but never, ever the night before the wedding. If you have any doubts about this, remember your worst hangover ever, then imagine being rousted out of bed to take vows in public in front of your and your fiancée's family. Your wedding day will be stressful enough without balancing a cold compress on your head.

Location. It is theoretically possible to throw a bachelor party in one of the ice-sculpture-type banquet rooms, but unless you're Frank Sinatra, it probably isn't a dream setting. Most men find it difficult to cut loose in a place where they serve pâté and the waiters drape little towels over their arms.

Host. The best man is traditionally the host, but in situations where the best man is from out of town, that becomes impractical. Anyone, including the groom himself, can throw the bachelor party.

Tuxedos. Don't wear your tuxedo to the bachelor party. While it may look great in the movies, when an actor spills something on his tuxedo, a little fat woman comes scampering out of a trailer with a replacement. Whatever *you* spill on your tuxedo will be in every wedding picture for the rest of

THE INSANELY GREAT BACHELOR PARTY MACHINE

I was just sitting at home,
> *planning a fabulous honeymoon,*
> *writing thank-you notes,*
> *thinking about love, marriage, and commitment,*
> *mastering differential calculus,*

when I heard the phone

ring. It was my
> *best man,*
> *best friend,*
> *brother,*

who told me
> *"your sister's in jail"*
> *"the big poker game is tonight"*
> *"the bank is giving out free money"*
> *"Springsteen's playing under a fake name"*

and he said

that I should drop everything and meet him
> *near an abandoned slaughterhouse.*
> *in a really bad part of town.*
> *by the iguana house at the zoo.*

I complained,

saying,
> *"Sorry, I have other plans tonight."*
> *"My fiancée is coming over."*
> *"I don't feel like it."*
> *"I'd rather have my teeth pulled."*

But my
> *best man*
> *best friend*
> *brother*

insisted, saying,

> *"You owe me a favor."*
> *"This is an emergency."*
> *"Don't be a wimp."*
> *"You're not married yet."*

So I go where he tells me, but as soon as I get there he starts laughing,

blindfolds me, and I was
> *locked into a car.*
> *forcibly taken onto a plane.*
> *forced to walk a long distance.*

And all the groomsmen show up, and

start laughing with him. I was terrified—what were they doing? When they removed the blindfold, I

was taken into
> *Harley Heaven Biker's Bar,*
> *an illegal secret casino,*
> *an abandoned prison,*
> *Nudie Judy's Party Room,*

which is filled with
> *ex-cons and gang members,*
> *the FBI's 10 Most Wanted all in*
> *one place,*
> *rednecks carrying shotguns,*
> *Elvis, Jimi, Janis, Che, Hoffa,*
> *and several more,*

all partying like it's the end of the world. My
> *best man*
> *best friend*
> *brother*

slaps me on the back and says, "It's your

bachelor party! He slides a big
> *zombie*
> *Long Island iced tea*
> *glass of grain alcohol*
> *beaker of blue liquid*

into my hand and forces me to drink it all at

once. Then, every tough guy in the place says he's going to buy me a drink, and I see laid out, end to

end,
| lots of liquor. |
| *a bodacious bounty of booze.* |
| *stupendous volumes of hooch.* |

So what can I say? We indulged. We toasted just about every-

thing, saying, "Here's to
| *your health!* |
| *your future!* |
| *tax, title, license, and options!* |

Then the lights came up, the door flew open,

and in came
| *six girls wearing three bikinis!* |
| *Miss March, Miss April, and all the months with no "R."* |
| *a women's gymnastic team, dressed for the locker room.* |

At that point, it gets a little

fuzzy. I'm sure we didn't do anything bad, though. We probably just . . . talked. After they left, and I

| *found my shorts,* |
| *scrubbed off the cooking oil,* |
| *bandaged up the welts,* |

all the groomsmen and I left the place, went across town, and

| *hotwired a steamroller and rolled through town.* |
| *dynamited a collection of pink flamingos.* |
| *soaped windows at the police station.* |
| *had a rumble with some Hell's Angels.* |
| *kidnapped a bull and locked it in a china shop.* |

It isn't clear what exactly happened after that, but

sometime the next morning I woke up
| *in a dentist's office.* |
| *in the back row of a porno theater.* |
| *in a moving freight car destined for Mexico.* |
| *in a dinghy floating in the city fountain.* |
| *in Cleveland, Ohio.* |

I heard the

terrifying noise of
| *barking dogs* |
| *sirens* |
| *shotguns* |
| *a missile countdown* |

and had a fistfight with
| *an armed guard* |
| *a judo champion* |
| *the Green Bay Packers* |
| *a murderous robot from the future* |

and won! My groomsmen showed up and got me out of there at the last second before

| *all hell broke loose* |
| *the place exploded in flames* |
| *the gunships came* |
| *I was killed* |

and they took me safely home.

And that's what really, really happened at my bachelor party—you can look it up.

your life, and in the year 2035 you'll have to explain to your grandchildren that the stuff on your tuxedo in the wedding photo is chili con carne.

While the bride gets the full responsibility and/or final say on many other events surrounding the wedding, she is specifically excluded from the bachelor party, a "no girls allowed" kind of clubhouse. Some view it as the last big fling, which wrongly implies that once you say "I do" you never have fun again. More correctly, it is just a bad-ass blowout with the boys, with lots of eating, drinking, swearing, and male bonding.

If your best man chooses to shoulder the whole responsibility, perhaps even surprise you with a bachelor party, you need only to let him know that it's not to be the night before the wedding. If, as is more often the case, you're in on helping plan the party, plan it with style, originality, and, most important, excess.

Weddings tend to be female-dominated rituals, and the bachelor party is the ideal antidote. At the rehearsal dinner, at the reception, when meeting your in-laws, and at all the other parties relating to the wedding, you'll have plenty of time to be refined and polite. The bachelor party is a time to be crude and rude.

Going bar-hopping or having a party in your best man's home are possibilities, but what makes an occasion memorable is doing something mindlessly macho and excessive and that's fairly original. A weekend of hunting, an all-night drive to Vegas or Atlantic City (if you live near either one), a camping excursion, or a trip to the race track or drag strip are excellent options. Higher-than-normal-stakes poker, a wicked game of mud football, a ski trip, or a jaunt to every down-and-dirty rock-and-roll bar in the city also make good bachelor parties. About the only option not worth considering is anything that could be considered elegant or in good taste.

AMERICAN STOCK PHOTOGRAPHY

HIDDEN TRAPS

Is it possible to screw up throwing a bachelor party? Following are some pitfalls that have occurred in the past:

Eric, a 29-year-old Oregon groom, was pleased when a close friend offered to throw him a bash at the friend's apartment. He had counted on some wild times and good conversation (including some swearing, of course). Once he got there, Eric realized that (a) it wasn't strictly a bachelor party, in that there were dozens of women there; (b) some of his groomsmen hadn't been invited; and (c) at 10:00 P.M., an hour into the festivities, he found himself in a room full of total strangers. When the host planned the party, his brain went on "autopilot" and he just went through the motions to throw a "party," forgetting totally about "bachelor."

Whoever plans the festivities has to be aware of the distinction between a bachelor party and any other occasion. A bachelor party, by definition, is a *men-only* affair, like a locker room or an electronics store. If it's not at someone's home, the choice of venue should be a place that no woman would want to go to anyway—like a boxing match, or one of the city's finer mud-wrestling establishments. The bachelor party is supposed to be in honor of the groom, so he should know and like everyone who is invited, and everyone he wants there should be asked to attend. In addition, there should be a sense of exclusivity about the bachelor party—the idea is to *get away from other people* for a few hours, not to have a huge generic wild party.

Ted, a Texas groom, was taken out by his brother, along with all the groomsmen in his party. They went to Red Randy's, a local rock-and-roll club where Ted's favorite band was playing, and his friends paid for the food and drinks. The only problem was that it was the same club that Ted and his friends went to almost every week of the year, and they ran into the same people they always saw and did the same things they always did. To this day, Ted cannot remember much about his bachelor party, not because of any extreme abuse of

INSANELY MACHO DRINKS

Alcohol consumption is not a prerequisite for a good time, but if you are going to drink, you may as well do it wrong. At your bachelor party, why ask for a wimpy glass of fine white wine or some kind of yuppie beer that's served with a lime, when instead you could guzzle down a Suffering Bastard chased by a Kamikaze? The following deadly concoctions came from the righteous brothers of the TKE fraternity at the University of Southern California, who know how to throw an outrageous party.

Long Island Iced Tea: Vodka, gin, rum, tequila, Coke, and sweet and sour.

Zombie: Orange juice and five types of rum. The true connoisseur feels cheated when they only use four kinds of rum.

Kamikaze: Vodka, Triple Sec, and lime juice. Might wipe you out, but gets the job done.

B-52: Kahlua, Grand Marnier, and Bailey's Irish Cream. Note to younger readers: Besides being a rock group, B-52s are bomber planes that you may see on the evening news.

Stealth Bomber: Vodka, gin, tequila, pineapple juice, and soda. You can't see it, you can't hear it, but it always hits its target.

Screaming Orgasm: Vodka, Bailey's Irish Cream, and Kahlua. A good detail for the stories you tell . . . "And then, at midnight, when the girls were hanging from the chandeliers, I had a Screaming Orgasm!"

Suffering Bastard: Triple Sec, orange juice, champagne, and light and dark rum. The name becomes more comprehensible the morning after you've had several of these.

substances, but because it was so much like every other visit to Red Randy's.

The bachelor party should be more exotic than any other night out on the town. If you wait till the last minute to plan your party, it'll probably be pretty dull. As Weird Al Yankovich says, "Dare to be stupid." This is a party that can happen only once. Make it memorable.

GROOMS WRECK CARS, TOO

If you're going to drink, *make sure that someone else is driving*. Everyone should know that by now, with the national media sounding the call every twenty minutes or so, but some guys feel that "just this once," on the night of their bachelor party, they'll be magically protected from the law against drunk driving, and from the law of physics that says two objects cannot occupy the same place at the same time (e.g., your car and a Mack truck). Lots of weddings have to be postponed because the groom is serving a mandatory three-day jail sentence for driving drunk, and some ceremonies are delayed indefinitely when the groom wraps a car around a telephone pole. *The only thing worse than a hangover on your wedding day is a coma.* The police don't care if you're getting married, nor does the judge, nor do the laws of physics. It's *a good thing* to be extremely foolish and irresponsible during your bachelor party, but *not on the highway*. Have someone sober do the driving.

12

COLD FEET

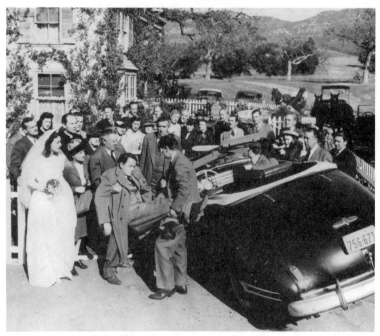

AMERICAN STOCK PHOTOGRAPHY

t's three weeks before the wedding. Your "unattached" male friends are going to a local club to scope out the babes and don't invite you. The cost of the wedding, the honeymoon, and the deposit on your new apartment have whittled your checking balance down to the point where it would comfortably fit in a piggy bank. And you just got into an argument with your fiancée—it began over whether you could put the autographed Guns N' Roses poster in the living room, but degenerated into a free-for-all that seemed to cut to the heart of your value system. And you don't even care that much about Guns N' Roses.

That night, you wake up in a cold sweat—a wicked voice whispering into your brain, "Don't do it, man!" You wonder if you would be having more fun out with your friends, instead of at home, looking at pictures of tuxedos. A lot of little things that have happened since you got engaged are starting to appear ominous. The conspiracy theories leap out at you. Are you settling down, or getting tied down? Is marriage a doorway, or a trap? *Are you making a big mistake?*

What about the things your single friends said? "We're gonna miss you, guy!" and, "You used to be so much fun to be around," and, "Wow, getting married! No woman will ever catch me! I always knew you'd be the first." Were they congratulating you to your face, but laughing behind your back? Were some of their comments more appropriate to someone who was terminally ill?

151

And what about Betty Lou Abernathy? You broke up with her five years ago (and have always thought she was a bitch), but now you wonder, *What the heck ever happened to Betty? Maybe she mellowed out.*

How about the "lone wolf" image? Don't you think you can handle things by yourself, one man against the world, a combination of Ernest Hemingway and Humphrey Bogart, ready for anything, anytime, anywhere, the kind of guy who talks plain and keeps things simple and doesn't owe nothin' to no one?

If these kinds of thoughts plague you, you are suffering from cold feet. Please do not become alarmed. Breathe normally, and return your seat to its full upright position. Your emotions will soon return to normal. Premarital jitters are par for the course. The time to worry is if you *don't* have any doubts.

Marriage is a big decision, a turning point in your life, and just like that first day of kindergarten, or your first serious job, it can occasionally seem like a pitch-black abyss waiting to swallow you whole. It's not.

Let's reexamine the facts:

1. The *lone wolf* business is almost all hype created by losers who just can't get along with people and like to pretend they're on their own by choice. After all, Ernest Hemingway was the world's premier proponent of the loner life, and he blew his brains out. Humphrey Bogart's "one man, one gun, one life" image was only for the movies. In reality, he was happily married to Lauren Bacall.

2. *Your single buddies* have to keep going out cruising for babes simply because they haven't yet gotten their acts together enough to land one for good. Behind your back, they're not laughing at you. They're crying tears into their beers, wondering how you can be so lucky. Everyone wants to find true love—you have, and they haven't. They're not going to come out and say, "You're right, I'm wrong. I don't have what it takes, but you do." The little cracks they make are often more from envy than contempt.

3. That terrifying image of the *pitch-black abyss waiting to swallow you whole* popped into your head simply because you thought about the future. Don't. If you want to contemplate a *really* depressing future, think about ten years from now, putzing along in the single life the same way you are now, but with more body fat and less hair. The future always looks grim; many guys never think about the future at all until they get married, and then mistakenly believe that it's marriage that's scary, when in reality the future is what's scary, single, married, or living in a hermit colony. *Cure:* Don't concentrate too hard on the future. The best weather predictions that modern man has been able to devise project about two weeks. The furthest you should be worried about is more like two and a half weeks.

4. *Betty Lou Abernathy* has picked up quite a lot of weight. Her voice went up several octaves and is currently the vocal equivalent of a dentist's drill. She's selling Mary Kay products in Detroit, not very successfully at that. To tell you the truth, Betty Lou hasn't thought about you since she found your favorite album in a box last December, shortly before giving it to a nasty neighborhood kid who used it as a Frisbee.

CAUSES FOR JITTERS

Fear of Getting Old

Marriage is a major mental dividing line, and you may think that married people are "old," and you're a "young" person.

Fallacy: Ask yourself this: Will staying single preserve your youth? Can a man keep a 17-year-old's outlook and attitude indefinitely? Would he want to?

Go find someone ten years older than you who's still single, and ask him what he's done in the last ten years. Chances are, not much. One is hard-pressed to find a more bitter, depressing SOB than an old guy who feels that his whole life would have been worthwhile if only he had landed the right girl some years back. The sad thing is that those who gripe about a missed opportunity for love are usually right.

Watch out for men in bars who ask, "What the Sam-Hill makes you want to get married? I never did, and I'm a better man for it today."

You can often find one of these basket cases nursing a drink in a hard-drinking kind of bar, a place with a neon sign that says Dog & Suds Bar & Grill, with half of the lights missing so it reads, Do & Su s Ba & Gr ll. *"Louise said, 'Marry me, Al, or I'm a-leavin' you,' way back in '63. I thought hard, and said, 'Go ahead, leave'—never thinking she would. And what do ya' know—she packed up her things the next day. Now she's living in Washington with some retired TV repairman who gave in to her. Well—you know what I got over that TV repairman—I got my freedom, yessir, free-dumb. I'm free to come in here every night and wonder what my life woulda been like had I a-married Louise."*

"Tears in their beers" guys aren't always so forthcoming. A lot of times they redirect their failure to act into false pride. In other words, they pretend to hate all women, having blown their chances with one (or a dozen). The "women—who needs 'em?" guy might be at the Dog & Suds, or he might just spend all his time doing macho stuff. You know, four games of racquetball every day of the week, rock climbing on weekends, building all of the "Wordless Workshop" projects in *Popular Science*. Lots of free time, but not by choice. *"And I like it that way,"* he'll lie.

Perspective

A lot of prewedding jitters are due to the many things that occur simultaneously before a wedding. Besides the obvious, getting married can include meeting lots of strangers, reflecting on your past, moving, taking time off from work or school, spending lots of money you may not have, talking/dancing in public, tangling with the clergy, and being near the center of attention for a little while.

"I felt like a pinball bouncing against bumpers," said Tom, a student in Louisiana. Tom was spending all his free time handling wedding stuff, and three weeks before the big day he was nearly exhausted. The final straw was when he found out that all his out-of-town guests' reservations had been accidentally canceled due to computer error.

He had planned to go bicycling that afternoon, and discovered that instead he would be spending the day arguing with sullen hotel clerks. "I was furious. I started thinking the unthinkable—what if I throw in the towel? Then I sat down and realized I still wanted to marry Beverly. It was only the hassles that annoyed me, not the marriage." He laughed. "Then I went down to the hotel and vented my spleen. They gave me new reservations for better rooms, and tossed in two for free." Tom figured out quickly what some grooms never learn. Isolate the source of aggravation and stomp it to death. Don't let a series of petty setbacks cloud your attitude toward getting married.

The *process* of getting married is a hassle, just like the *process* of getting a driver's license is a hassle. Once you can drive, though, you never think about the gory "Blood on the Pavement" films you had to sit through, the idiotic driver's-education classes, the mystery of the stick shift, or even the lines at the Department of Motor Vehicles. All those hassles are forgotten in your first drive down an open road.

In the same way, the hoops you have to jump through in getting married will be forgotten soon enough. As the good Dr. Martin Luther King said, "Keep your eyes on the prize." You don't necessarily have to *enjoy* every little obstacle on the way, but it's important not to become overwhelmed by the hassles, either. No matter what goofball situations you find youself in, just keep telling yourself: *I only have to do this once.*

SOME QUESTIONS APPREHENSIVE GROOMS HAVE ASKED IN THE PAST

Will I Turn into Fred MacMurray?

The father figure of the late twentieth century, Fred Mac-Murray embodies all the archetypal qualities of middle-agedness: He's sensible, well mannered, and a little befuddled at the wacky antics of the youngsters of the world. Some grooms fear that after they say, "I do," a goblin will hop out from behind the altar, force them into button-down sweaters, stuff pipes in their mouths, and forbid them from ever raising their voices again.

In its time, Fred MacMurray–ness was on the cutting edge. However, husbands are different every generation, and it is unlikely that you will turn into Fred MacMurray, *unless you want to*. Fred MacMurray phobia grows out of the unfounded belief that it was family life that turned Mr. MacMurray into a genteel fellow with a pipe. The truth is that he was always like that.

Will I Miss My Single Days?

Yes. You may miss being single, but only in the same way as you miss high school and living at home. As John Cougar Mellencamp said, to "stay seventeen as long as you can" is some people's goal. As you grow older, *regardless of whether you're single or married,* you will miss "the old days."

Maybe you miss high school—but flunking your senior year over and over again until you died would not preserve your fond feelings of Whateveritwascalled High. You'd just feel stupid. Maybe you miss living at home with your parents—but they weren't going to make your breakfast and clean your clothes till you were 50. In the same way, you can hang on to all your good feelings about your single days, at the same time realizing that to prolong them would be disappointing.

A flirty waitress, a cute girl on the train to work, or even a sexy-sounding telephone operator can excite feelings of cold feet in a guy about to get married. *I wonder what I might have done in this same situation a year ago,* the anxious groom-to-be wonders. Wonder away. It's a year later, and just as going back to high school would be ridiculous, it's absurd to imagine being a wild and crazy single guy again. Women* have a saying: All of the good ones are taken. Well, that makes you

---

*And Warren Zevon

Getting married can be hassle—but so can getting a driver's license. Once you can drive, though, the grief of driver's ed is quickly forgotten.

IS GETTING MARRIED LIKE GETTING A DRIVER'S LICENSE?

Before getting your driver's license . . .	Before getting married . . .
You have to watch a lot of gory films of bad car wrecks. The moral is supposed to be, "Don't crash like these fools," not, "Don't drive at all."	You have to hear a lot of recently divorced men tell you bad stories from failed marriages. The moral is, "Don't be a jerk like these fools," not, "Don't get married at all."
You learn that with the added speed and luxury of driving come some additional responsibilities, but that it's all definitely worth it.	You learn that with the joy of having a lifelong partner come some additional responsibilities, but that it's all definitely worth it.
At some time in the learning process, you panic, and feel you're about to be smashed to smithereens. But soon you overcome your fear, realize the enormous benefits of driving, and think it's ridiculous to be scared of driving, and never give it another thought.	At some time before you get married, you panic, and feel you're about to be smashed to smithereens. But soon you overcome your fear, and realize the enormous gains to be had in marrying such an amazing woman. You realize it's ridiculous to be scared, and never give it another thought.
You have to submit to a lot of legal rigmarole, culminating in passing a test, taking your birth certificate down to the courthouse, and making it all "legal."	You have to submit to a lot of legal rigmarole, culminating in passing a blood test, taking both your birth certificates to the courthouse, and making it all "legal."

Before getting your driver's license . . .	**Before getting married . . .**
After it's all over, you realize it's great to drive, and would never have it any other way. All of the hassles you encountered on the way are quickly forgotten as you enjoy driving.	After it's all over, you realize it's great to be married, and would never have it any other way. All of the hassles on the way to the altar are quickly forgotten as you enjoy married life.

one of the good ones. Not a bad thing at all. Just smile, and think to yourself, *You might want me, but you can't have me.*

What If My Wife Turns Out to Be a Space Alien?

As the grocery-store magazines point out, this happens quite often, especially in England. If your wife *is* a space alien, you should learn to love her for what she is. If you just think she's extraterrestrial, but have no hard evidence, such as seeing her levitate or remove her head, seek out a good therapist.

13

THE
HONEYMOON

As you get close to the wedding day, the burdens of family, moving, and taking care of the business details of getting hitched can all but choke the romance out of your relationship. With the changes you're enduring, arguments with your fiancée can become a daily gauntlet, as the dainty rose of your romance is run over by the Sherman tank of premarital stress.

Rick, an engineer from Minnesota, was a quiet, stay-away-from-the-crowds kind of guy, who got engaged to Marilyn, a telephone operator from his town who shared his fondness for backpacking and watching movies on tape at home. During the month before their wedding, Rick got ten years' worth of the things in life he disliked most—meeting crowds of new people, going to parties and dinners, and using up most of his energy playing "Mr. Junior Politician" as he met Marilyn's extended, rather loud, family.

After several weeks of packed rooms and outstretched hands, Rick wanted to turn down just one party and spend a quiet day with Marilyn. She argued with him: "We have to go—it's my aunt and uncle from Texas, and they've come up just to see us!" Rick went, but the seed of doubt had been planted in his mind: *This is not the woman I thought I got engaged to.*

When they were dating, *before all this wedding stuff,* it had been a running joke between Rick and Marilyn, after accepting an invitation to a party, on the drive over to pretend to get lost and instead rent a movie, order some take-out Chinese food, and spend the evening by themselves. It may have been rude, but it was romantic, and it was the kind of impulsive togetherness that Rick loved. *Now,* thought Rick, *Marilyn is hell-bent on going to every soirée that comes our way.* In reality, he'd rather have chewed off his own leg than go to another party, but Marilyn insisted.

After yet *another* evening of answering, "What do *you* do?" and having nosy relatives try to figure out how much he made, and telling the same damned, surefire funny stories, he talked to Marilyn about how she'd changed. "You didn't used to want to go to every party we were invited to. Remember when we used to get 'lost'?" To his surprise, Marilyn laughed, and shouted, "I wish we could skip all these things too! I hate 'em!"

Rick was delighted that Marilyn felt the same way he did. She told him, "I wish we could pick up our backpacks, go way out in the woods by a stream, and sit on a rock. Like for a week. No phone, no cars, and no people—except you." And that was what they did for their honeymoon—they left directly from the ceremony in Rick's Jeep, changed into jeans and flannel, headed for their favorite campsite in northern Minnesota, and vegetated together. It got their marriage off to a good start and gave them plenty of time to catch up with each other.

During the inevitable bickering and hassles, it is crucial to remember that *the situation is causing the trouble—not your fiancée.* The typical groom may ask himself, "What happened to that girl I used to date?" and the best antidote to such wedding-induced battle fatigue is a little R & R with the woman you love. A honeymoon is a great way to find out that she's been there all along. The real reason to take a honeymoon is to rediscover the romance that brought the two of you together, and to put the maddening trauma of your wedding behind you.

Your honeymoon doesn't have to cost thousands of dollars, nor is it necessary to take three months off work. The primary objective in planning a honeymoon is to enjoy a little time together, doing whatever the two of you like most, away from the difficulties of daily life. Think of your honeymoon as the biggest date you'll ever go on. It's the groom's responsibility to come up with a good honeymoon strategy, and he should be creative, thoughtful, and inventive while planning it. The most obvious and gaudy honeymoon destination—two weeks of seclusion in a cabin by a palm tree at the beach—is *not* necessarily the best for you.

The shrewd groom, before ordering brochures or talking to travel agents, will first take inventory of what he and his bride like to do most. Are you an "outdoors" couple, into camping, hiking, and exploring nature? Or do you prefer the excitement of urban life, catching the newest movies and eating at foreign restaurants? The advice of your older brother, who told you about *his* great honeymoon in Florida, might not apply to you and your wife, especially if your wife hates beaches. It's *your* honeymoon, and it should be exactly what you like to do.

TALK TO YOUR BRIDE!

Although the groom is the point man for the honeymoon, he should consult heavily with his bride before planning anything. No matter how well you think you know her, it's possible to really screw things up on the honeymoon if you don't solicit her advice. Eight great European cities in eleven days might be the perfect adventure for you, but to your wife, who had hoped to get a sunburn by a pool somewhere, it could appear to be a living hell of suitcases and smelly diesel buses.

Lee, a groom from Tennessee, was getting married for the second time, as was his wife, Tammy. Lee thought it would be a great idea to keep the honeymoon destination a secret from Tammy until they were on the road, and he did some groundwork to find a great resort in the woods of Georgia, where they could just be together, ride horses, and relax. Tammy tried very hard to find out ahead of time where they were going, but Lee kept it a secret. Driving away from the chapel, he still wouldn't tell her, and it wasn't until they were just a few miles from the resort that he told her the hot spot he'd chosen.

Tammy looked as if he'd hit her. "It's a great place!" he insisted. "It's got all the things we like—horseback riding, walks in the woods, our own little cabin—what's the matter?" It was too late when Lee learned why he should have consulted her earlier. "This is the same resort where my first husband took me for a honeymoon," Tammy said, forcing a smile. Lee was dumbstruck—of all the possible things that could go wrong, that was the only one he had never considered. They went anyway, and had a pretty good time, but the memory of her first marriage haunted Lee the whole vacation. He wished he'd asked her.

Even when you're both getting married for the first time, there are plenty of good reasons why you should consult your fiancée on your honeymoon destination. It's *her* vacation, too, and she deserves a say in what you do. Remember the wisdom of Lyndon B. Johnson: "The secret to a successful marriage is first to let your wife believe she's having her own way, and second, to let her have it."

WHERE TO GET INFORMATION ON HONEYMOON DESTINATIONS

After consulting with your fiancée about the general nature of your destination, it's your assignment to find the actual place. This may be the most fun wedding planning of all. The first rule is to *plan it as far in advance as possible.* Wherever you want to go, other people want to go there too, and places fill up. Don't hope that you can throw something together in the week before you get married. There's a good chance you'll find disappointment.

A pretty good source of information is in the back of bridal magazines. Usually, the last fifty pages are nothing but advertisements showing happy couples standing hip-deep in giant soap-filled champagne glasses. If you fill out the reader-reply card, in a matter of weeks you can find yourself inundated with apparently glamorous honeymoon destinations.

Once you've thrown out the ones that are just too expensive, far away, or awful, you may still have several dozen locations to consider. Don't use the bridal magazines as your only source, however; the literature you receive is *advertising* and thus will always make a place look better than it actually is. Many of the vacations advertised are undoubtedly wonderful, but you should consider other sources for two reasons: (1) to get independent confirmation that your choice for a honeymoon is the "perfect" place; and (2), so that you can find a spot where you will not be confronted by dozens of other lovestruck honeymooners at every heart-shaped Jacuzzi.

A travel agent can be a great help in picking a good spot. Travel agents charge you no fees, collecting only from the airlines and resorts for which they book.

Travel agents are independent—they make a commission on whatever trip they book for you, and they'll be as straightforward as anybody about what they recommend, since they don't have a stake in any particular company. If you have a good idea what you want to spend and approximately what kind of honeymoon you'd like, travel agents can prepare an agenda that fits your needs exactly.

HONEYMOON BUDGET

The prices for honeymoons vary tremendously, and even two trips to the same spot can have wildly divergent costs. When looking at a "package" trip, you have to take into account all of the following costs:

- Travel—whether by plane or boat, or automotive expenses if you drive.
- Meals—some packages include breakfast, some include all meals. If you're going to a city, try to find out the prices of typical restaurants in that city.
- Taxes—some hotels quote a price over the phone that does not include sales tax, or special "room" taxes that are tacked on. These room taxes can be as high as 15 percent.

- Service charges—some resorts and hotels, especially in foreign countries, automatically tack on a 15 percent service charge to your total bill. This can upset your budget considerably.
- Entertainment—what are you going to do? Are sports, movies, side trips, and so on included in the package cost? If not, how much extra are they?

If you're choosing a package trip, before plunking down a fat deposit based on a glossy advertisement and a toll-free telephone call, the shrewd groom should investigate the reality of any resort or hotel by calling them directly and asking some tough questions. Calling in the middle of the day will often get you a hotel P.R. rep, who will field all questions with answers rehearsed to make the place sound better than it actually is. Calling the hotel directly late at night can sometimes connect you with the night auditor or graveyard shift desk clerk, who may be more candid about the realities of the hotel.

Some questions to ask:

- Besides the advertised price, how many extras are added to the bill? Do they charge two dollars per telephone call? Is there a sales tax, room tax, automatic service charge, or any other hidden cost? Is the cost advertised per *person,* or per *room?* If it is per-person (a disturbing recent trend in pricing), the actual cost may be twice as high or more.
- How quiet is the hotel? Ask if there's any nearby construction, a freeway or busy street, or even an airport. Hotels are often near airports.
- How many different classes of rooms are there? Sometimes, an advertisement will show the deluxe room, and have copy listing rooms priced "from" $49.95. The cheaper rooms might not have the view, or may be smaller than the room pictured. Package tours are often able to offer low prices because the hotel can fill the unwanted rooms with groups.

A sk: Is the honeymoon destination you chose quiet?

- What "freebies" come with the reservation? Sometimes, prices include all meals, and even wine. Other resorts may include VCRs in the rooms, recreation such as golf or tennis, and tours of local landmarks. If there are enough free extras, a room that seems expensive may actually be a good value.
- When there are no freebies, ask what you can expect to pay for meals in the hotel. Get the lowest and highest prices for entrées, and the same for wine (if you drink).
- Ask what's in the immediate neighborhood of the hotel. Is it on the beach? In the woods? Are there other restaurants, movie theaters, museums, et ceterea, nearby?

If you choose to have a romantic vacation for two (and can afford it), remember that what looks good in the ad may not be so wonderful once you get there. "Truth in advertising" is almost a contradiction in terms—just look at the 1950s ads for "healthy" cigarettes, or today's pitches for "good-tasting" light beer. You should view ads for vacation getaways with the same skepticism.

Carl T. (do you really care whether it's his real name?) skimmed the ads in the back of a bridal magazine several months before getting married, and made reservations at a "secluded mountain resort" that catered to newlyweds. The ad contained the most attractive photo, a smiling couple toasting each other with champagne in front of an ornate fountain. It promised "complimentary champagne in our new- lywed suites" and "limousine from the airport," and it seemed like the perfect place for Carl and his bride, Donna, to begin married life.

After the wedding, the couple flew to the town near the resort. The advertisement had been so beautiful that on the day Carl and Donna arrived, so did around twenty-five other newlywed couples. Nothing in the ad was specifically false— the "limousine," actually a mini-van with the words LIMO OF LOVE painted on the side, picked them up at the same time as three other couples.

The "resort" was secluded—thirty-five miles out of town in

the mountains. What wasn't secluded were the guests. The hotel had two hundred rooms, one small pool, a Jacuzzi, and a restaurant/bar. Since there were no other restaurants nearby, "seclusion" meant that Carl and Donna had to eat in Top o' the Woods for breakfast, lunch, and dinner.

They did get free champagne in their room (a four-dollar value!), and the fountain with a bed of flowers behind it was at the hotel, just as the ad had promised. What the ad didn't show was that in front of the fountain, out of view of the carefully composed photograph, was a construction site, with a sign that read COMING SOON—THE LOVE WING, which rendered it a spot devoid of romance, in addition to bringing noisy construction crews every morning at seven o'clock.

In spite of it all, Carl and Donna did have fun, had lots of time to spend with each other, and found it easy to get up early and grab a good spot at the pool thanks to the wake-up call in the form of a noisy construction crew. What they learned was the meaning of "marriage mills"—resorts set up as honeymoon factories, churning couples through like so much "product." The advantage of these places is that they're easy to find and often will cater to your needs fabulously. The danger, of course, is that being surrounded by other new-lyweds can make what should be the best vacation in your life seem like a common experience. The staff of the hotel, jaded by dozens of couples every day, can sometimes treat you like just two more customers.

Ads and agents are the obvious route, but if you're a creative kind of guy, you *can* put together your own special honeymoon. First, go to your local bookstore, which usually has a whole section devoted to travel planning. (You know exactly where you want to go, you just don't know that you do.) At the bookstore you will find amazingly specific books: *Country Inns of California; Beautiful Beaches in New England; Tiny Sweaty Apartments in Hot Southern Towns.* Some travel books are independent of the resorts that they cover and will candidly list the advantages and disadvantages of one place over another, rating the view, weather, entertainment, food, quality

How about a wonderful cruise for two?

of the staff, and so on. Advertisements in magazines present only the one-sided view of the resort. Even if you have your heart set on a destination you've seen in an ad, it is worthwhile to verify the information in a travel book.

Vacation planning does not require the mental capacity of a "Jeopardy" champion. Use the "Honeymoon Budget Form" (see page 177) to compare the prices, desirability, and cost of a variety of locations, then make your pick. More than any travel agent, your friends, or your big brother, you know what would make a good honeymoon for you and your bride. Taking the ball in your own hands and running with it can provide more satisfaction than any other, wimpy route.

HONEYMOON DESTINATION	WHAT TO LOOK FORWARD TO	WHAT TO BEWARE OF
Package tours	You can know ahead of time how much you'll be spending, since package tours often can give you a flat rate for everything—airfare, meals, accommodations, even (occasionally) free souvenirs. This makes it easy to plan for in your budget. Many package tours include entertainment such as swimming, boating, golf, and side trips to local hot spots.	Package operators often sell unwanted hotel rooms to unsuspecting groups, which could land you overlooking the construction site *behind* the beachfront hotel. A package tour may be overpromoted, so that the secluded, private getaway they promised is actually packed with hundreds of other people looking unsuccessfully for solitude, who share the twenty-minute twice-a-day Greyhound bus trip to the "conveniently close" beach.

HONEYMOON DESTINATION	WHAT TO LOOK FORWARD TO	WHAT TO BEWARE OF
Bed-and-breakfasts	These quaint, homey retreats can often provide solitude far away from the maddening crowds. The personal touches added by the owners, who usually live there, can give these retreats a unique charm not found in a hotel chain. Some B & B's are in locations as exotic as beautiful old Victorian homes, lighthouses, and isolated ranch houses. A great B & B experience can be a private cottage with its own fireplace, overlooking a majestic bay, or a room in a charming old hotel in the middle of a large metropolis.	The owner who was so friendly when you first arrived can become annoying after a couple of days. Since you're actually staying in someone's *home*, you have to be civil to the owners, who may not leave you alone. Since every bed-and-breakfast is a private business, quality varies wildly, and amenities such as your own bathroom are not always offered. Some owners are downright paranoid about taking care of their places and will give you a list of dos and don'ts more restrictive than staying with your grandmother! In addition, being away from the crowd can also mean being away from restaurants, beaches, and any form of entertainment other than Chinese checkers offered by the owner.

HONEYMOON DESTINATION	WHAT TO LOOK FORWARD TO	WHAT TO BEWARE OF
Honeymoon getaway specialty retreats	Far from being "marriage mills," many of the resorts catering to new-lyweds can actually offer everything in one romantic place. Since they have dealt with thousands of other sweet young couples, they know when to leave you alone. Sexy extras like heart-shaped two-person bathtubs, champagne in the room, and "breakfast all day long" appeal to those who want to start their marriage with a bang.	Being surrounded by other newlyweds can give a "mass-produced" sense to your fantasy, and occasionally the staff acts as if they couldn't care less. Some people consider champagne-glass-shaped bathtubs downright silly, and some resorts are isolated in such a way that you have to buy all meals, souvenirs, and entertainment at a premium from the hoteliers.
Exotic foreign destinations	It can be exciting to visit a faraway country while enjoying the first days of marriage, and some couples opt for Europe, Australia, or another overseas destination. Being thousands of miles from home can give you and your wife a real sense of to-getherness, exploring the wonders of another culture.	In addition to the high cost, and the necessity for shots, passports, and visas, the shock of visiting another country is not always pleasant. The fact that *they don't speak English over here!* is often a traumatic discovery, and two weeks without Doritos and Oreos is for some the essence of sacrifice.

HONEYMOON DESTINATION	WHAT TO LOOK FORWARD TO	WHAT TO BEWARE OF
Beach resorts	Two weeks on the beach! Nothing to do but eat, sleep, and sun! To many couples, this is the essence of romance, and there are dozens of excellent getaways that provide this luxury.	Day 4 of 14—your wife is sunburned, but it doesn't matter because it's raining anyway, and you were both sick of lying in the sand. You've already seen the movie at the only theater in town, and the restaurant is closed on Sundays. Some beach resorts offer *nothing else*, and for any extended stay, that can be deadly.

It sounded perfect in the brochure they sent us.

AMERICAN STOCK PHOTOGRAPHY

HONEYMOON BUDGET FORM

____ Air travel for two (round trip)
____ Gasoline
____ Hotel room including room tax (____ days × $ ____ per day)
____ Breakfasts (____ days × $ ____ per day)
____ Lunches   (____ days × $ ____ per day)
____ Dinners   (____ days × $ ____ per day)
____ Entertainment
____ Car rental
____ Spending cash(____ days × $ ____ per day)
____ Miscellaneous (suntan lotion, snacks, etc.)
____ Sales tax
____ Service charges, if any
____ TOTAL

When comparing prices on package tours, use this form. Some resorts seem to have higher prices, but upon closer examination they may include taxes, meals, or entertainment that you'd have to pay for at other destinations.

THE AT-HOME HONEYMOON

It doesn't take prodigious piles of cash spent on a cruise ship to have a good honeymoon. Remember that you mainly want to spend time together, away from the maddening crowds. Many a couple has enjoyed a honeymoon at home.

The successful at-home honeymoon is predicated on making home as fun and romantic as possible. Following are some tips for a home honeymoon that will make Club Med pale by comparison:

1. Your first task is to keep other people away. An active "disinformation" campaign in the months before the wed-

ding can accomplish that objective. Don't let a soul know about your plans to stay at home. Instead, drop hints to friends and family that the two of you are planning a trip to a faraway place. The "fib" honeymoon destination should be as believable as possible; it helps to fool nosy friends if you leave brochures lying out where prying eyes can get the wrong idea. The topper in misleading hints comes when you pack a suitcase—this will fool even the shrewdest snoop.

2. Supplies: A couple of days before the wedding, stock up on the things you'll need, so that you don't have to leave home unless you really want to. A partial list of essentials includes:

   - Candles—extremely important!
   - Clean sheets, clean towels, clean clothes, clean dishes— in the crush before your wedding, you may run low on clean laundry. You don't want to be doing the wash on your honeymoon, so beg or bribe a friend to "catch you up."
   - Groceries—get her favorite foods, your favorite foods, and some wine, soda, and snacks. No diet can't be broken in the name of love, so get some good chocolates, too. Strawberries, apples, and other fruit can be fun to eat together, even while kissing. If you don't want to cook, get some cold chicken or other ready-to-eat good- ies.
   - If you have a VCR, rent a bunch of your favorite movies, including the first one you ever saw together—even if it was a terrible movie. If you have a stereo, get a recording of her favorite band, even if you can't stand them. She'll love you for it.
   - Some good bubble bath, and your favorite cologne, might come in handy . . .

3. Execution: When you're leaving the wedding, make sure you aren't followed. Take a circuitous route around the city if necessary, maybe even stopping at lover's lane for a little postmarital necking. (You'll be happy to discover it's still just as fun.) Head home. Hide the car. Unplug the phone.

Light the candles. Open the wine, and look across the room at the woman you love. . . .

4. DON'T ANSWER THE DOOR! Whoever it is, they can wait.

SMARTNESS BOX
Let's Not Get Pregnant Right Away

One of the highlights of any good honeymoon should be lots of postmarital sex. Unless you want to find yourself reading *The New Dad's Survival Manual* real soon, the subject of birth control has to be considered.

Modern science has provided a wealth of birth-control options, from the intrauterine device (which sounds like something that would be used on *Star Trek:* "Captain—set the intrauterine device on stun!"), all the way down to the ancient and simple condom. None of the choices will do any good if you don't use them.

You may just hope that your fiancée will handle the birth control; you may feel it's too "icky" a subject to broach; and you may end up shopping for diapers within the year. Don't wait till the wedding night to find out that nothing has been done. Discuss the subject with your fiancée, and plan ahead. Some options, such as a diaphragm or "the pill," require a doctor's prescription, and others carry a high risk of failure. Your local Planned Parenthood chapter can usually answer any questions, and a visit to them as a couple can provide straight answers to sensitive questions.

If you totally wimp out, and plan just to hope she's done the work for both of you, a good backup is to throw a couple of boxes of condoms into your suitcase. Make sure they're regular contraceptive condoms purchased from a drugstore: the ones sold from coin-operated machines in gas stations are usually marked FOR AMUSEMENT ONLY—NOT INTENDED FOR USE AS A CONTRACEPTIVE. Just ignoring the subject or hoping it will go away could be detrimental to your sex life.

14

THE
BIG DAY

The Big Day: Above all, look, listen, and enjoy the day. This is not a dress rehearsal.

G round Control, we are T-minus five hours and count-ing. All the months of planning and preparation are directed toward one end—the day you exchange vows with the woman you love. To strangers, your wedding day will be a twenty-four-hour period like any other, and they'll work or watch TV or maybe invent a better mousetrap; it's hard to believe it's just another day. But then again, the *Apollo* launch was just another day, too.

Houston, prepare groom for launch. If you think you might be anxious on the day of your wedding, enlist your best man to calm you down. Tell him in no uncertain terms that he's to provide backup support for you, to fetch you candy bars, or just to stand around and tell jokes. The morning before the wedding can be a lot of fun, and some grooms prefer not to have anything formal planned for those few hours. It may be the only unstructured time till the honeymoon is over, and it provides a good opportunity to catch up with friends and family.

T-minus two hours—Mission Control, execute final check. Before leaving, go over the last-minute business details with the best man. Give him the payment for the officiant—cash in an envelope is best. Give him the rings. Explain all the business details before leaving, and tell him to keep track of things and not to bother you with them again. That's what your best man is supposed to do. It's his job, and you have better things to think about than business.

T-minus ninety minutes and counting—Mission Control, transfer groom to wedding site. Have the best man drive— that's his job, too. Take the best space in front. It's okay, today. Check in with the wedding officiant. He'll be relieved to see that everything is going according to plan.

T-minus sixty minutes—Mission Control, begin seating guests. The ushers should be in place, ready for guests to arrive. Long ago, they should have been coached about who sits where. The groom is usually stationed away from the excitement. Keep your best man handy, to keep you entertained.

T-minus five minutes—Prepare for liftoff. Stand by. Get a last drink of water.

If your entourage is the pushy sort, last-minute advice may start pouring in at an alarming rate. If you're prepared for that to happen, it won't faze you, but if you're caught off guard, it can blow your head clean off. People will suddenly start dumping on you all kinds of things they've heard: "Black the bottoms of your shoes so if you kneel they'll look good to the congregation"; "Kiss her with a big, showy bend-her-backwards kiss"; "Kiss her gently, don't lean her backwards"; "If someone wears white (black) it's bad manners (bad luck)"; "You're wearing the wrong kind of clothes"; "If you see the bride before the ceremony, it's bad luck"; "What if someone objects in that part in the ceremony where they can?"; "What if you pass out?"; and so on. You get the picture. Just don't be caught off guard, and each time someone suggests something, no matter how outrageous, just thank them, smile, say, "Good idea," and immediately forget about it.

WHAT IF (God Forbid!) SOMETHING GOES WRONG?

The real question is what to do *when,* not if, something goes wrong, because no matter how much preparation and planning goes in, something is bound to foul up. Murphy's Law applies to weddings, too, and the best a groom can do is to maintain his composure, realize, *Now I know what went wrong,* and stay with the program.

The *only* real goal of the wedding day is to marry the bride to the groom. Although a small fortune may be spent tacking on accoutrements to this simple task, the only thing that can *seriously* go wrong is if at the end of the day you and your fiancée aren't husband and wife. However, if you set your expectations too high, such as planning to have a *perfect* ceremony and a *perfect* reception and *perfect* groomsmen and bridesmaids, then you are sure to be overly worried at first, and then disappointed later. Following are a variety of possible problems that could occur, coupled with solutions.

Ring Trouble

Even after receiving the advice and pestering of every friend and relative in the hemisphere, and going through every published wedding-preparation checklist in the United States, some people still find ways to have trouble with the rings. What could happen at your wedding?

Groom #344, Phoenix. "The heat and my bride's allergies made her fingers swell up. The ring wouldn't go on her ring finger." Solution: He put it on her pinkie. No one blew up, and he's still just as married to Mrs. 344 (née 194).

Groom #1012, Minneapolis. "In the excitement of the moment, I put the ring on her right hand instead of the left." Solution: Later, he swapped it around and had a good laugh with his new wife. Groom 1012 is just as married anyway. The mystery of hand-switching isn't all that complicated. Due to a quirk in the quantum mechanical reality of the post-Einstein comprehension of relative time and space, a woman who is facing you actually reverses polarity, i.e., her left hand is on your right, and vice versa. Memorize this. Learn quantum mechanics. Read *A Brief History of Time* without really understanding it. And after all that, if you do accidentally put the ring on the wrong hand, don't sweat it. Justify yourself by claiming it was a tiny tribute to *glasnost;* in the Soviet Union, wedding bands always go on the right hand.

Groom #60609, Chicago. He experienced the biggest, most terrifying ring problem of all, and lived to tell about it: "Um, the best man forgot the rings. He'd put them in his suit pocket before changing into the tuxedo, and forgot to switch them." Groom #60609 is also just as married as if nothing had gone wrong, although his best man was from that moment on known as the "merely adequate" man. *Lots* of people forget the rings. Although you won't, thanks to the excellent preparation regime you will undertake (yeah, right), if you want to worry about "what ifs," just do what #60609 did: He and his bride were momentarily embarrassed, but they completed their vows without the rings, and later had a special ring-exchanging ceremony at the reception. Then they threw the "merely adequate" man into a pool.

What If . . .

. . . *I muff a line?* Say it again. This is extremely common, and nothing major to worry about.

. . . *The bride is late?* Wait for her. What're you going to do, say the vows by yourself?

. . . *An important member of the bridal party (besides the bride) is late?* Wait a little while. Then go ahead without the straggler. It's her tough luck, not yours.

. . . *My outdoor ceremony is rained out?* First, go inside. Then, get married. It's good luck to have rain on a wedding day, by the way.

. . . *The officiant gives a long and embarrassing sermon about what's wrong with young people nowadays?* This is a more common occurrence than members of the clergy would like to admit. If it is a religious ceremony and the clergyman is planning to give a sermon, ask him ahead of time what the topic will be. Careful selection of an officiant can usually avoid this problem, but in many churches, you get whomever you get. Try to dissuade him from ranting about the sorry state of the world, or about how many people get divorced nowadays. If the speaker unexpectedly goes off on an ugly tangent, just tune him out until he gets to the part about you and your bride. One Philadelphia bride went so far as to ask her rabbi to stop midsermon, and he did.

. . . *We have a weather crisis?* Snowstorms, power outages, and floods all make exciting wedding stories a couple of years after the fact, but at the time it can seem as if nature is against your union. In inclement weather, just remember: Get the bride married to the groom, and watch the storm.

. . . *Our car breaks down?* Get a ride.

Stage Fright—And What to Do About It

According to a variety of surveys that ask people what they fear most, "speaking in public" is always included as one of the scariest possible activities. It's possible that "wedding nerves" could merely be garden-variety stage fright, and there are excellent strategies to mitigate any fears you might have.

1. Remember that nobody is even going to be looking at you. The star of this show is the bride, and the director is the rabbi, priest, minister, or judge who runs the show. As annoying as it may be to find out that you have become a bit-player in your own wedding, you probably realized it long before the wedding day. Being second fiddle is a distinct advantage in curing stage fright. *Note: Do not let your bride think about this. If she suffers from stage fright, this will only aggravate her condition.*

2. Understand that a little bit of stage fright is a good thing. On this important occasion, the groom should not saunter out to the altar as relaxed as if he just woke up. A little bit of nervous energy can go a long way toward making the day memorable. Relaxing too much can destroy the heightened awareness that comes only on rare occasions like weddings, graduation days, and the days when the Chicago Cubs win.

3. If you're still nervous, try this exercise recommended by acting teachers: If possible dim the lights in the room. Sit down and close your eyes. Inhale, then exhale slowly. Inhale, then exhale slowly. Repeat for two or three minutes. The exhale is more important than the inhale, and this simple

system seems to work quite well. If you fall asleep, you've gone too far.

4. Stage fright cannot be cured by drinking. Although you may *feel* less nervous after a good stiff drink, it is an illusory sensation. You would merely turn yourself from a nervous groom into a drunken nervous groom—twice as much trouble for everyone. Stay off the brew till you say "I do."

ENJOY YOUR WEDDING DAY

Once you've admitted that *something* will go wrong, cured yourself of any stage fright, and handed off the business details to your best man, it's up to you to enjoy your wedding day. This simple and important observation about attitude is often overlooked.

Enjoying your wedding day doesn't mean that you have to be a blithering idiot, telling bad jokes and entertaining all of those around you; rather, it's a personal decision to savor the details of something that will happen only once. When your beautiful bride walks down the aisle, *look at her*—mentally record the moment. No photo of the event afterward can duplicate the impression you get when she comes toward you, with people looking on and the music playing. When she gets up to you, subtly greet her—take her hand, or just make eye contact with her. Try to be conscious of the feel of her hand and the smell of her perfume. The most memorable details of the day are the ones you can experience—you're not a spectator watching the Super Bowl, you're the quarterback.

Sixties philosopher Wavy Gravy (people took weird nicknames then) had a saying: Be Here Now. Although Mr. Gravy may have been inspired while using illegal drugs, his words can be taken to heart on your wedding day. One New York groom put it this way: "Even after all the hassle and logistics before the wedding, once they started playing 'Here Comes the Bride,' it really was like magic." There are few such moments in a life, and the primary contribution a groom can make on the Big Day is to forget about all his problems and let the magic run its course.

Be there. Listen to the vows, and think about what you say as you repeat them. Although many couples write their own ceremony, it's not necessary to change one word for the ceremony to be truly personal. The words that have been exchanged for generations are elegant, direct, and take a new meaning when you say them to your bride. Brandon, a Texas lawyer, is quite accustomed to addressing large groups of people. However, he reported that on his wedding day, "I said the vows very quietly, directly to Carla. I held her hand, and looked her in the eye, and said them *to her*. I was marrying Carla; not all the other nice folks in the church that day." When your bride says her vows, listen to what she's saying. No matter how many times you've heard the vows before, they'll be poetry on only one occasion in your life.

Once the magic starts, little can go wrong. No matter what happens, it will become a part of your wedding-day stories to be told for years to come. If you simply make the decision to enjoy your wedding day no matter what happens, you'll be an excellent groom.

15

THE
RECEPTION

No matter whether the ceremony went off without a hitch, or if every possible thing went wrong from rain to forgetting the rings, you've accomplished the primary objective—you've made the transition from an engaged couple to husband and wife. The pressure is now off, and what follows is essentially a big party. Party down with your new wife!

To celebrate the new marriage, there is considerable ritual to the reception. After photos at the church or at the place where the reception will be held, there's typically a reception line, toasts, dancing, cake cutting, tossing of the bouquet and garter, and then making your escape. Unless you were raised as the son of an ambassador, most of these "formal party" activities may seem a bit alien and can be intimidating. With a little cunning and know-how, "formal" partying can be as much of a blast as knocking back a few brews with your buddies.

THE RECEPTION LINE

After the wedding, the reception line provides an opportunity for everyone to greet and congratulate you and your wife (may as well get used to the term now) and "receive" you into the world as a married couple. If you basically stand there and smile, shaking the men's hands and hugging the women, you won't go too far wrong. At a large wedding the reception line may be the only opportunity you have to speak to many of the guests, so making each little bit of small-talk personal will score major points with all involved. Rather than shaking hands like a robot politician and repeating, "Nice to see you, so glad you could come," over and over, try dredging something specific to each person out of the recesses of your overworked mind. "Mrs. Baker—thanks so much for your help when we were apartment hunting"; "Cousin Fred—I always see you at weddings. Betcha didn't expect the next one to be *mine!*"; and so on. Don't drag it out, though—if there's someone you want to talk to at length, wait at least till everyone is through the reception line.

There may be a fair number of faces you don't recognize, people who know your name but you don't know theirs. It's perfectly legitimate to ask their names, and an excellent piece of small-talk comes from the inevitable trying to sort out where they fit in. "Oh, you must be Esther's daughter-in-law! I've heard so many good things about your Franklin Mint collections!"

The difficult spots are those people whom you should know but whose names you've forgotten. Nick from Toronto married his childhood sweetheart, Jenny, who came from the exceptionally large Weatherby family. Jenny had enough uncles and cousins to pack a chartered bus to their wedding, and Nick had met many of them over the years. However, their names and faces all sort of ran together in Nick's mind, but he pulled out a technical victory by merely greeting them more enthusiastically than ever, and quickly pulling out any anecdotes he could remember. "It's so nice to see you! I remember the time Jenny and I visited your farm!" That way, they knew he had remembered them, even if he couldn't call them by name.

Another hint for remembering names is to carefully listen to your bride, who comes before you in the reception line, and see what she calls each person. One of the more helpful traditions is for each person in the receiving line to introduce the next guests, but if your party doesn't do it, you have to resort to quick-wittedness combined with eavesdropping.

TOASTING

You can appear to be a silver-tongued devil even if you've never spoken in public in your life. When the champagne or whatever is broken out, usually the best man makes the first toast to you and your bride. You and your wife (used to that word yet?) sit that one out—i.e., you don't drink to yourselves—then you propose a toast to your bride. What do you say?

Gush. In most other situations in your life, you're expected to speak modestly, in careful, hedged terms. But this is your new wife, so you'll appear sweet, sensitive, and loving if you fill your toast with superlatives. It doesn't even have to be long. "To Sheila, the most wonderful and beautiful girl in the world, and the best bride a guy could ever dream of." For those hams who want to go for the extralong toast, it doesn't hurt to think about it a little bit in advance. Try telling about how you met— "When I first met Sheila, we had both just jumped into a cab and wanted to go in opposite directions. But I quickly decided I'd go wherever she was going—and I haven't looked back since. . . ." But always end your toast with a little gushing anyway, because it really plays to those back rows. ". . . Here's to the most beautiful, smartest, funniest girl I ever jumped into a cab with!"

Watch out for toasts that are too funny. Living as we are amid the great Irony Epidemic, every guy across the nation thinks he can be David Letterman. Self-deprecating humor may be appropriate on late-night television, but when you're making a toast, you should be expressing a genuine, heartfelt emotion, not telling a stupid joke. Thus, avoid sentiments like, "I know she ain't no rocket scientist and she's sure as hell not Miss America but she said yes so I'll take her." It's not the time or place for that kind of thing.

Other toasts. After the big toasts by various members of the bridal party, there may be spontaneous toasting throughout the party. You can appear as eloquent as John F. Kennedy by simply remembering a used-car-salesman's trick. The word most pleasing to just about anyone is his or her own name.

So, you can rattle off some prizewinning toasts by merely looking around you and mentioning the people you see, stringing their names into reasonably decent sentences. "Here's to my new family, the Joneses, and especially *Mr. and Mrs. Jones,* who brought *Sheila* into the world!" Later, try, "Here's to *Don* and *Earl* and *Fred* and *Pete,* some totally excellent groomsmen." And so on. It doesn't matter too much what you say, as long as you get the names in. Don't forget your parents, her parents, the best man, and the maid/matron of honor. They'll love you for it and comment for years afterward about what a fine speaker you were.

DANCING

Earl and Lois, who ran a mail-order business in Topeka together both before and after their wedding, had always loved to dance. "Trouble was," said Earl, "our taste ran more toward Concrete Blonde and The Smiths than to Chopin, so our main dance step was the modified hugga-hugga." Lois wanted a "big band" at the wedding, to give an air of late-forties' class to the festivities, and they knew they couldn't hugga-hugga for their first big dance as husband and wife. "We looked into taking dance classes, but there was just no time to do it. So we practiced faking a box step of our own invention while listening to some of our favorite records. It fooled the crowd at the wedding."

When the reception includes lots of "real" dancing, your options are (a) learn to dance, or (b) like Earl and Lois, learn to fake it. If you practice some sort of serious-looking slow dance with your fiancée, you'll probably be fine for that first song, to which the bride and groom dance alone.

A good wedding coordinator has a whole checklist of dance partners for you and your bride—you'll have to cut a rug at various times with her mother, your mother, the maid of honor, and so on. The man is expected to lead (i.e., know how to dance), and especially with older partners, they expect you to move them around the floor. "But I just wanted to get married! I don't want to be Fred Astaire!" you complain. Here are some tips on faking out a *real* dancer:

You can learn to dance like a pro, or just have fun pretending. Even if you don't know a waltz from a tango, it's easy to learn how to fake it.

1. Always start with the right foot. In American dance, that's how things are done. If your mother-in-law is English, she may want you to start with the left, because the English have it backward, just like they drive on the wrong side of the road. But in every other case, you'll be expected to start with your right foot.

2. Position your feet between your partner's feet.

3. Hold on to your dance partner with your right arm around her back, your left holding her hand away from your bodies.

4. Finally, you have to move. Just make an attempt to discern the rhythm of the music, and take steps forward, right, left, back, forward, right, left, back, and so on. Hold your partner firmly enough that you move her with you. The essential thing is that the man is leading, and you have to make your partner go where you go, no matter how improbable. You're in charge, and if you move around confidently enough, a good dancer will follow. A bad dancer won't care one way or the other.

5. Don't step on her feet. The easiest way to avoid this obvious faux pas is by keeping *your* feet as close to the ground as possible without shuffling, and by moving slowly enough that you don't kick her in the foot.

Most important:

6. Talk a blue streak. If you're babbling away—"I'm so glad Uncle Don could come, I really like your corsage, it's raining cats and dogs in Nebraska, blah blah blah"—your dance partner will probably not even notice that you have absolutely no idea what you're doing or where you're going. Thank her after the dance, and smile graciously. You'll get away with murder.

CUTTING THE CAKE

At a military wedding, the cutting of the cake is invested with some macho flair by using the groom's saber (sword) to cut the first slices. At other weddings, there's often a special decorated knife for the slicing. Then you feed her a piece of cake, and she feeds you one.

Alessandro, a Bronx groom, almost precipitated a hasty divorce by taking his cues on postnuptial cake feeding from the movies. It can't be emphasized enough how unlike real life movie weddings are, since Alessandro chose to use a tactic appropriate only to the Marx Brothers and shoved a huge chunk of icing-laden cake into the face of his new wife, Martha. She contained her anger for the moment, but he saw the message in her eyes—*What the hell are you doing, you mindless jerk?*

He forgot to consider that Martha, like most brides, had spent months of preparation to look perfect for the occasion. She had a dress handmade by her aunt, a new hairdo, makeup hastily purchased at the last minute at great expense, and now this philistine (who also happened to be her husband) was smearing cake onto her face, spilling it on her dress, and making her look goofy in front of everyone she knew. It is impossible to underestimate the importance that your bride attaches to appearances, especially on the day she gets married. Martha didn't deck him right there, but she did scold him when they got back the pictures, and she will tweak him about it every time they pull out the photos until he dies.

So—consider appearances. If you want to be funny, save it for the throwing of the garter, an opportunity to clown around that won't smear anyone's makeup. Another word on garter throwing: The tradition goes that the man who catches the garter will be the next to get married. Even though this superstition holds no more water than the belief that walking under a ladder will give you bad luck, people seem to believe that the garter catcher will get hitched, just like most people will walk around a ladder. If the single men at your reception have the irrational fear of marriage that is common nowadays (*"What, me? Get married? The ol' lone wolf? Never!"*), the garter throwing may be a complete fiasco, as it was at the reception for Derek, a young engineer. "I threw it, and instead of an eager rush to get the garter, all my friends were kind of backing away, like it was the plague. After the garter sat on the ground with everybody staring at it, a friend of mine finally halfheartedly picked it up, and the band ended the drumroll that seemed to go on forever."

No matter how many of your friends claim not to be superstitious, and no matter how many others say they're not scared by the prospect of getting married, you may find that every single one of them has decided to "just let the others" fight over the garter. The resulting inaction can be quite conspicuous and embarrassing. The solution? Tell your best man to instruct as many of the men as possible, in advance, that they are to fight like wild animals for the garter, or be prepared for immediate and severe reprisals. It might even help to sweeten the pot a little by having a prize for the man who gets the garter, such as a little trophy, or, as in the case of one California couple, a flask of liquor that the bride had stowed in the garter.

MAKING THE GETAWAY

The party may seem like it's just hitting its stride when you and your bride have to leave. Don't worry too much about that, because that's how it always seems. After your new wife (like the sound of that?) throws her bouquet, you can change into traveling clothes and take off. A crowd of well-wishers will follow you outside and cheer as you leave. If you're drunk, get someone else to drive. Or arrange for a classy exit some other, more exotic way. Claudia and John, an Ohio couple who were married in downtown Columbus, hired a horse-and-buggy usually used for tourists to take them away from the church. Claudia loved the ceremony—it was a scaled-down version of the way Princess Diana left her wedding.

If you take your own car, be prepared for the shock of wedding decorations covering your vehicle from hood to trunk, and tin cans and shoes rattling behind you. The purpose for this tradition is to ward off evil spirits. Whether or not you believe in evil spirits, in order to ward off state police, drive a suitable distance from the church, then cut off the cans. It helps to stow a knife in the trunk before the wedding. Save the noisemakers: they make fun souvenirs, and the tradition in some places is to hang the shoes and cans from the door of your new home when you come back from the honeymoon, a way of bringing a little of the wedding home with you.

16

MAKING THE TRANSITION FROM TRANSITION FROM GROOM TO HUSBAND

The honeymoon is over when he phones that he'll be late for supper—and she has already left a note that it's in the refrigerator.

—Bill Lawrence

After getting back from their honeymoon, Harley and Dorothy, both corporate trainers, were greeted by a number of messages on their phone machine, from their offices, from credit-card companies, from people they'd borrowed things from, and from people who didn't even know that they'd just gotten married. The scariest message of them all was from Dorothy's office, left by a manager who said, "Okay, kids. The party's over. I have a crisis here at work and need you to call back as soon as you get home." It saddened both of them a little bit: Life does return to its normal, boring pace after the honeymoon, and the wedding decorations and cards all over their apartment looked as out of place as Christmas decorations left hanging in February.

How to keep the magic in your marriage is a subject about which dozens of books and hundreds of articles have been written; however, by the time someone reads one of those books, there's already a problem. The better course of action is one of preventive maintenance—28.35 grams of prevention being worth .454 kilograms of cure, metric-wise. Have realistic expectations. Don't take your wife for granted. And react to problems in the proper perspective.

REALISTIC EXPECTATIONS

Weddings are happy occasions. Being a newlywed is a joyous and exciting thing. However, some otherwise sensible people are a little disappointed to find out that being married isn't just one happy, smiling face after another. The only surefire, guaranteed method for staying happy all the time, married or single, is a frontal lobotomy. Most doctors, however, no longer perform lobotomies on demand, so the new husband has to pursue alternative methods for keeping his life on track.

Wanting to be happy all the time is significantly different from expecting to be happy all the time. If you expect instant Ozzie and Harriet–style domestic bliss the minute you start your new life, little problems will have a way of getting blown out of proportion. A burned dinner, a missing toothpaste cap, or a night in which your new wife wants to go out with her friends without you, all can seem ominous to someone who has his sights set on correcting all the wrongs in his life the day he begins married life.

Getting married means that you have a fantastic, wonderful woman whom you love very much and with whom you will share your life—a pretty good arrangement, and something to be pleased about. However, it doesn't mean that you no longer have bills to pay, work to do, car trouble, or toothaches. It doesn't mean that you'll get serious about weight lifting, finally learn French and FORTRAN, write the great American novel, or get better at chess; you won't end all the long-term fights with your relatives, you won't get a promotion at work, and you won't win a Nobel prize. A part of the unrealistic expectations that new husbands sometimes have is, "Now that I'm getting serious about love and marriage, I'm going to be a more serious person."

Having shattered any unrealistic expectations about yourself, what about your wife? Here are some common questions new husbands have, and the answers:

QUESTION: Will my wife become a great cook, housekeeper, and social maven now that we're married?

ANSWER: No.

QUESTION: Will my wife stop seeing those friends of hers whom I can't stand?

ANSWER: No.

QUESTION: Well then, in fairness, doesn't my wife finally have to take a liking to those friends of mine whom she can't stand?

ANSWER: No.

QUESTION: Will my wife learn to dance and play piano, lose some weight, and quit drinking/smoking/stuttering/ saying "ain't"/holding her spoon wrong at the dinner table?

ANSWER: No.

QUESTION: Will she please, *please* stop playing Barry Manilow (or *that record*) around the house?

ANSWER: No.

The fact that she said "I do" doesn't grant you any right to try to change your wife into another person. Your wife was around for at least eighteen years before she married you, and any belief that "she'll change once we get married" is extremely unfair to her and unnecessarily stressful on your relationship. The good part about being married is that you're two *different* people, and the husband who keeps himself sane revels in those differences, rather than trying to stamp them out. After all, if your wife were exactly the same as you, then you'd be married to a man. *Gross!*

APPRECIATING YOUR WIFE

Lou, a Miami, Florida, chemical engineer, pondered what seemed to be a failure in his married life: He felt that his sex life, and his love life in general, had lost its spontaneity. "When we were dating, there was so much romance floating around. I really felt it then—we might have a date, and decide to skip work the next day and go on a trip somewhere. Now that we're together all the time, we hardly ever do that kind of spur-of-the-moment thing."

Lou's gripe comes from a misconception coupled with a missed opportunity. The misconception is that single life was more spontaneous than married life. Single life is anything but spontaneous. A good date usually begins a long time before: Dinner reservations are made, concert tickets are purchased, and all week long the man and woman make sure everything is in place for the "perfect" evening—shirt pressed, a haircut, and cologne for the man; makeup, a new dress, and perfume for the woman. And then they have the perfect evening, during which supposedly spontaneous good times happen.

The perfect romantic good time, upon close examination, was less than spontaneous. Hours of planning and, equally important, anticipation went into it, and once a couple is married, they can't forget about the planning and anticipation. A part of appreciating your wife is to treat her as if you still have to win her over—constantly.

DATE YOUR WIFE

Lou's missed opportunity was in not putting the same kind of care and thought into his married romance as he had done in his single days. It's not the restaurant that makes for the perfect date—it's the planning and anticipation. Once a husband realizes that he cannot make everyday life an endless parade of good times, it's up to him to get a little cake to break up the meat-and-potatoes of existence.

Get in the habit of planning good times periodically—it's not necessary to wait for a birthday, Valentine's Day, or a three-day weekend to do something special with your wife. When you were first dating the woman who became your wife, chances are you were always scouting for an opportunity to invite her out on a date. That's a good instinct, and one that shouldn't stop, ever.

Good times don't have to be expensive or fancy—a picnic, a drive in the country, getting some movies and ordering pizza, or even cleaning up the apartment (without her prompting), all make for excellent romantic evenings. What is often overlooked is that you should give your wife some advance notice. Springing flowers on her and saying, "Drop everything, we're going for a night on the town," can be as jarring as not doing anything. For women, sometimes looking forward to a nice night out is as much a part of a romantic evening as the event itself. You can get more mileage, more romance, and a better time by telling her on Monday that you'll be going out Friday. That way, she can look forward to it all week, and she gets an opportunity to plan for it herself. Once you've put a lot of time, effort, and strategy into seducing her, spontaneity can finally happen.

HAVE AN AFFAIR WITH A MARRIED WOMAN

A couple of months after he got married, Don, a factory supervisor, started splitting right after work a couple of nights a week, skipping the traditional after-work beer with his friends. His co-workers wondered where he was going, but Don just smiled mysteriously and said, "I'm meeting someone." A couple of times he called in to work and said he was sick, but then when they called his house to ask a question, no one answered.

People, being as nosy as they are, started talking about his strange disappearances, and finally had their suspicions confirmed when Don skipped a lunch invitation and came back smelling of perfume and with lipstick on his collar. Knowing that Don had just gotten hitched, a gossiping friend of his didn't exactly follow him (he said he was "just going the same way"), but did see him leave the plant and pick up a woman in his truck. When the co-worker passed him on the freeway, he was shocked and amazed to see that Don was with . . . his wife.

Under all the pressure of daily life, Don had found that his free time was quickly whittled away, with the demands of work, friends, and relatives; his wife, Dee, had discovered the same thing. So, for their romantic thrills, they discovered that occasionally they had to sneak around—not on each other, but on their friends. When Don tried to go about it the regular, above-board way, he found that it was hard for people to accept that he was going to miss a night of bowling or a dinner invitation in order to be with his wife. So he went the mysterious route: He would just do it, and not let anyone, friend or foe, on to exactly what he was doing.

Now that you're married, it's high time you started having an affair. The kind of steamy, secretive relationship with a married woman that requires you to cancel appointments, invent excuses to get away from faces who might recognize you (or your date), steal a few precious minutes away from all those who would have you do otherwise. The good part is, the married woman of your desires is none other than your new wife.

Affairs can consist of a particularly heated month of naughtiness, or a periodic liaison that is renewed in those rare moments when both parties can sneak away from their obligations. If you can put the energy and dedication into your relationship with your wife that some sleazier men put into illicit affairs, it can only strengthen the bond between you.

Dating your wife and having periodic affairs with her are all a part of continuing to respect her. The woman who married you shouldn't come to believe that "When a girl marries, she exchanges the attentions of many men for the inattention of one."* You should remember that she, more than anyone else, is worth bending a few rules for.

PERSPECTIVE

A very important rule for making the transition from groom to husband is to keep some perspective on things. In addition to being the object of your desire, your new wife is also your roommate, your personal business partner, and your friend. With all the different levels at which you'll relate to her, some fights or disagreements are inevitable, and the best way to deal with conflict is to look at it plainly and on its face.

_____

*Helen Rowland

Your Marriage, Your Life

Some experts advise that you should "work at your marriage as hard as at any job." Others have written books about "keeping the fun" in marriage, and would have people turn their married lives into one nonstop party. Both attitudes neglect the fact that no one's life is always the same, and that being married is neither all work nor all fun.

Making rules for how a marriage "should" work and specifying the "proper" behavior of both partners down to the last detail can only lead to disappointment. Just like life itself, marriage is constantly surprising, always changing and growing, and will rarely follow a formula.

Making the transition from groom to husband begins when you begin to make decisions (large and small) with the criterion of how they will benefit *the two of you,* rather than just considering yourself. At first it takes conscious effort to think that way, but soon it becomes second nature.

The vows that many couples recite include the words "for richer, for poorer; in sickness and in health." Taking those words to heart, and applying them creatively, can help a marriage endure every situation that may occur in life. As important as it is to stick together during the trying times, it may be even more important to enjoy the good times together. Live your married life fully and sincerely, and drink from life's deeper waters.

I leave you with the traditional salutation given a bride and groom:

Congratulations to you, and best wishes to your bride.

THE GROOM (AND HIS FAMILY) PAY FOR:
Wedding and engagement rings for the bride
The marriage license
Clergyman's fee
Bride's flowers
His own clothes
Boutonnieres for the best man, ushers, and himself
Flowers for the mothers/grandmothers of bride and groom
The rehearsal dinner
The honeymoon
A wedding gift for your bride

THE BRIDE (AND HER FAMILY) PAY FOR:
Everything else! Including:
Invitations
Her dress
Flowers for church, reception, bridesmaids
Photographers/videographers
Groom's ring
Gift for the groom
Reception: including food, drink, entertainment, and the
    wedding cake
Note: These lists merely represent tradition. Wedding expenses in the real world can be divided in any fashion that seems fitting.

COUNTDOWN TO MATRIMONY

T-Minus Six Months, or as Soon as Possible
Set the date for the wedding
Make a budget
Choose a location for the ceremony
Choose a location for the reception
Decide on the number of guests
Meet the clergyman or other officiant

T-Minus Three to Six Months
   Finalize guest lists: gather addresses
   Choose best man, groomsmen
   Begin planning honeymoon
   Help bride organize reception, including catering, entertainment, and renting a hall
   Get measured and order what you'll wear; ensure groomsmen do the same
   Register a gift list
   Send announcement to papers
   Order invitations/stationery

T-Minus Two to Three Months
   Finish addressing invitations
   Choose a florist
   Start planning rehearsal dinner

T-Minus Six Weeks
   Mail invitations, and don't look back
   Help with thank-you notes
   Help make seating charts
   Finalize plans for rehearsal dinner
   Order gifts for groomsmen
   Double-check with florist
   Check with formal-wear dealer to ensure your groomsmen have clothes ordered

T-Minus Four Weeks
   Get the marriage license
   Chase down invitees who haven't responded
   Confirm all services once again

T-Minus Two Weeks
   Get a great haircut
   Pick up the rings
   Help your bride to write thank-you notes and to generally stay sane and happy

T-Minus One Week
    Pick up gifts for groomsmen, bride
    Finalize guest lists
    Have bachelor party
    Reconfirm reservations for out-of-town guests
    Reconfirm with florist that flowers for bride, mothers/grand-
        mothers, and your groomsmen will be ready and deliv-
        ered to the proper location
    Test fit any rented clothing

T-Minus One Day
    Pick up formal wear
    Rehearsal
    Rehearsal dinner
    Try to get a good night's sleep

The Big Day
    Get married. Have a happy life.

ABOUT THE AUTHOR

MICHAEL R. PERRY is a free-lance writer living in Southern California. He edits an environmental newsletter, and has written magazine articles on a wide range of subjects, including music, motion pictures, and computer technology. Additionally, he has produced numerous educational and music videos through his company, C.U. Productions. Mr. Perry is more than happily married. He is currently completing his first novel.